WHILE PATROLLING BACKWARDS

Reminiscences of a Career Immigration Officer

By Andrew L. Hattery

ILLUSTRATIONS BY P. B. MOSHER

WHILE PATROLLING BACKWARDS

Andrew L. Hattery

Published by: Village Books, 1200 11th Street, Bellingham, WA 9822.
Copyright by Andrew L. Hattery - 2013 (alhattery@comcast.net)
Cover Illustration & Characterizations by Bruce M. Mosher
Cover Development by Julia Moquin
Edited by Robin Casale Fillman, PhD
Printed in USA
First Printing 2013
ISBN: 978-0-615-81575-6
Library of Congress Control Number: 2013909479

Dedication

To my loyal wife, Leona, who has been by at my side, through it all, for over 52 years.

Acknowledgments

"Con muchisimas gracias" to my niece, Robyn D. Casale Fillman, PhD, who encouraged me to write my recollections for the family and her graciousness in volunteering to edit my efforts in this endeavor.

My daughter, Melanie Ann Hattery Haines and her daughter, Julia Moquin, my niece, have been invaluable with their technical expertise and the polishing up of the finished product.

And, to talented Bruce (P.B.) Mosher, my friend of long-standing, for his cartoon renderings.

Introduction

Before my discharge from the Air Force in '57 my goal was to get a degree in accounting, ideally from a college in Idaho, and to obtain an associate degree with a transfer after two years to the University of Idaho. I did receive an associate's degree from North Idaho Junior College (now North Idaho College) in Coeur d'Alene, Idaho, majoring in business and accounting. But after one semester at the University of Idaho, my aspirations of becoming a CPA did not come to fruition. Getting married and starting a family brought me to the realization that supporting same was of paramount importance, and thus my successful career in the U.S. Immigration Service took root.

When I started college in February of '58 at least one third to one half of the student body was comprised of Korean War veterans on the GI Bill. We had a commonality and even a Veterans' Club. One of my veteran friends, who was not particularly cut out for academia, and tiring of college life, said that he had some Army buddies who were enjoying life in sunny southern California, having a great life, sharing an apartment with a pool. He suggested, "Why not take the written test for U.S. Border Patrol, there's no obligation." At this point in time I was into my second semester of college. I was still not bowled over about the idea of working on the Border Patrol. But what the heck, what did I have to lose? To make a long story short, I took my friend up on his suggestion and we requested the written test to commence the process. A month or so later we were taking the preliminary test to enter government service (it's hard to believe, but we were sitting across the room from each other when we took the test, and we made identical scores). What a test this proved to be - the majority of the questions concerned one's ability to pick up a foreign language. It proved to be the only test I have ever taken of which I wasn't sure of the outcome. By the time we were notified to report for physical examinations and an oral board, I was less enamored about the whole matter and did not show up for the final physical and oral examination. My friend flunked the oral examination and re-enlisted in the Army.

As to which I previously alluded, family obligations prompted me to have second thoughts about my career path. It didn't take long for me to realize that entry level accountants were making considerably less on the job than entry level border patrol positions were paying. And then, there were the "the perks": annual leave, sick leave, retirement, promotional opportunities, and job security. It seemed like a 'no-brainer'; my mind was made up! With little hesitation and with the affirmation of my wife, I notified personnel in Washington, D.C., which handled applicants for Border

Patrol positions that I was again interested, and in a short while I was set up for the required medical exam and oral board. Needless to say, I successfully passed all requirements.

In the early summer of 1961, I received notification to report for duty as a trainee Immigration Patrol Inspector at the Chula Vista Sector Headquarters located in San Ysidro, California, just across the border from Tijuana, Mexico. I entered on duty July 10th, leaving my wife and young son in Idaho to join me later in July. Interestingly, I have lost contact with my friend who apprised me of the great life of a Border Patrol officer. He is unaware that I was successful in pursuing the dream that he had.

Immigration Patrol Inspector

On July 10, 1961 my career began in the U.S. Immigration Naturalization Service as an Immigration Patrol Inspector. I was beginning to wonder what I had gotten myself into when I inquired of the less-than-helpful Greyhound bus driver in the bus station in San Diego if he knew of the Border Patrol station in Chula Vista, about 15 miles south from downtown San Diego. He said that as far as he knew, and he had been driving the route to the border for some time, he was not aware of any Border Patrol station located there. I finally resolved to take the bus anyway, and inquire at the bus station at the border at the predominately Hispanic community of San Ysidro, California.

Fortunately, a knowledgeable person was able to direct me to my place of employment, which was located on a hill or colloquially known as a mesa overlooking the sleepy, community of San Ysidro, California which was mostly inhabited by Latin Americans. As I recall, it was a beautiful, balmy sun-shiny day as I trudged, with baggage in hand, about ¾ of a mile up from the bus station to sector headquarters. I reported for duty, with orders in hand to be sworn in. Here I would spend the first four years and three months of my civil service career "guarding the border".

It didn't take long for me to realize that "guarding the border" was a very simplistic overview of the realities of my position. The authority instilled by regulation "to patrol the border to prevent illegal entry and arrest such entrants guilty of same" soon became reality: I learned that we had the even wider-ranging authority to question any person we believed to be illegally in the United States as to his/her right to be in the United States, and to make an arrest if necessary. Obviously, one needed to be quite astute in whom to question if their entry had not been observed. Being surrounded by so many individuals of Latino heritage (some of questionable citizenship), resulted in the establishment of probable cause difficult.

My wife, Leona and James "Jamie" Andrew joined me when they flew to Lindberg Field in San Diego about the 15th of July, 1961, where I picked them up. Leona immediately fell in love with the palm trees and the beautiful moderate weather. Jamie was just a little over one year old, and my wife was about 7 months pregnant. We had a little girl born prematurely on November 6, 1961, Denise Maria Hattery, who lived less than two hours. We had a short burial service for her at Fort Rosecrans Military Cemetery in San Diego. Several of our neighbors in San Ysidro attended. Even though her life was so short we will always remember her.

As to ferreting out illegal aliens, some officers were more zealous than others in their pursuit of a statistic. I am reminded of one afternoon that a probationary officer so proudly brought to the station several Hispanic family members whom he had accosted in the vicinity. He based his arrest on the evidence that their English knowledge was minimal, to say the least. After further investigation, it was discovered that the officer had not yet acquired the necessary Spanish language skills (pre-Border Patrol Academy) to question a person's right to be or to remain in the United States. It goes without saying that his bubble burst when an older officer with better Spanish language skills determined quickly that the persons that the young officer so proudly presented were permanent residents in the United States, and showed Alien Resident Cards for proof. To say the least, the young officer was embarrassed about the incident and he learned from it; naturally, good-natured ribbing took its course and over time to faded away.

In the early 1960s all officers ("Immigration Patrol Inspector" was our formal title) were required to attend the Border Patrol Academy for about 14 weeks. The Academy was an old WWII Naval station in Port Isabel, Texas was a quasi- military-style aggregation of barracks, mess hall, and sports field with the 'whole schmear' of uniforms, regimentation and bedcheck. As I was accustomed to military food from my Air Force experience, the food looked and tasted great to me. However, a student friend (who incidentally has been a personal friend of mine for nearly 50 years) had different thoughts about the food - it must have been the sheltered life that he had led prior to his entry into Civil Service. He was just ahead of me in the chow-line during breakfast of our first day at the Academy. Just behind the steam tables with his arms crossed was our cook in charge, resplendent with his chef's hat, looking very important and proud of overseeing his life's work. My friend proved to be the class wit, being exceptional at both, ad-libbing and being the center of attention, when he exclaimed, "This food is just like my mother made...." I looked at the cook as this was said, and I saw such a grin and a look of satisfaction on the cook's face, it was unbelievable. Then my friend finished his exclamation with "when she was drunk." Crestfallen, one could say of the cook's countenance, but it was even more than that; it was a look of derision. Not yet finished with his commentary, my friend said, as we got to the large commercial bread toaster at the end of the service line, "This toast reminds me that when I get back to Chula Vista I'm going to have to roof my house." I kept my mouth shut during this event (with maybe a slight grin on my face), so I had no future problems with the food. However, on subsequent visits to the chow hall, when this cook was on duty he would dig through the entrees and without fail locate the smallest pork chop, chicken, or whatever and personally serve him the smallest portion of whatever we had.

I would be remiss if I didn't mention this item about the food service at the Academy. It seems that one of my Catholic group (unsanctioned by us) went to the Academy Chief and mentioned the fact that a non-meat - specifically fish was not available for the Catholic students on Fridays in the mess hall. This suggestion did not carry much weight with the Chief and he as much as said "no dice!" This didn't stop the instigator. He placed a call to Robert Kennedy, then Attorney General in Washington, D.C. I still don't know how my classmate had the balls to make the call. Anyhow, the very next day the Chief called everyone to an assembly and in his apologetic preamble said he didn't realize there were so many Catholic students. So....from then on there would be both fish and meat on the menu in the mess hall every Friday. I only surmise that this was probably policy at the Academy from then on, at least when there was a Kennedy in the White House.

For the record, I have the deepest regard for the Academy Chief. We all were explicitly advised by wire that we were not to take our families to the Academy. Due to the fact that my wife lost our first-born girl within a few hours of her birth, just before my assignment to the Border Patrol Academy, my wife was in no way staying in Chula Vista or staying with her parents in Idaho during my training detail to Port Isabel. The Chief called me into his office when he found out about this arrangement and confided in me that he felt families should not be separated, but in case the Central Office got wind of my failure to obey orders, he would be able to explain. I never heard another word about the matter. Thank goodness the Chief was understandable and a good Christian family man.

Mine was the class of the 79th session, actually the second part of the first class to begin studies at Port Isabel, Texas. Previously the training had been conducted at Fort Bliss, Texas. It seems just like yesterday that the Chief and Deputy of the Academy, with their clipboards, made their rounds of the quarters at 11:00 at night checking on their charges. The curriculum was heavy on Spanish language, entailing a language laboratory and classroom work every day for about 4 hours. Other courses rounded out the curriculum, including Immigration & Nationality Law, Duties & Authorities to Act, First Aid, Fingerprinting, Alien Processing and the all-important firearms qualification, which remained a quarterly requisite during my Border Patrol years. Eight hour shifts on weekends were spent at the local stations and the patrol boat adding a practical aspect to our training.

Pistol training at the Academy started with .22 caliber weapons and graduated to .38 caliber at an outdoor range, where, I might add, the wind blew continuously making it difficult to hold on target. There is no doubt that if one could qualify there one could qualify anywhere. What I particularly remember about this phase of training was the instructor: an experienced and accomplished shooter and a member of the National Border Patrol pistol team, he was of medium height and swaggered when he walked. To look at him, one would say, "Now there's a pistol shooter." He had the requisite short muscular arms and strong shoulders that go with pistol shooting. When getting to the point, however, he was short on temper and he expected everything to go like clock-work. He stressed and re-stressed that our weapons were at all times to be pointed down range and the firing under his tutelage would be commenced with "ready on the right, ready on the left, ready on the firing range - fire". Heaven forbid if one wasn't ready to fire, and especially if a round fired without his command. His favorite saying in such a case was "my size 10 ½ shoe will be up the next person's ass that fires without my order." He was also known to say "Some of you guys handle a weapon like a bear cub handling his pecker for the first time," which in some way was a truthful observation. After shooting practice, the last hour of every day was physical training, unarmed defense, obstacle course and sports.

In order to retain employment as an Immigration Patrol Inspector, one was required to pass a 5 ½ month oral Spanish examination by Immigration Law Board and again at the end of 10 months of employment. The board usually consisted of a Chief Patrol Inspector, and several Assistant Patrol Inspectors. One member of the examining board would

speak only Spanish. The officer to be examined, who, I might add, was usually quite nervous, was furnished with 50 or so English questions. The examinee interpreted all of the questions in Spanish, then wrote the "Mexican" board member's replies in English on the question sheet. One was graded basically on fluency and grammar by the board. In my time, one got a 'pass' if they were not fortunate to have passed their 5 ½ month examination. However, a bona fide pass was mandatory at the dreaded 10 month examination. This examination was much more difficult; the questions were more complex, requiring long Spanish answers, and the subjunctive tense was added to the test.

The probationary period was one year. It cannot be overstated that while this was a nail-biting experience, to say the least, one was also quite apprehensive about employment; even passing the orals and written law would not guarantee a job. All during one's probationary period of one year, a trainee was evaluated bi-weekly by a journeyman officer. These evaluations consisted of a written explanation covering the trainee's progress and were called Conduct and Efficiency Reports (C&Es). Employment termination could result if a trainee were the recipient of too many reports of inadequate performance on the C&Es, even if the academics part of one's training were commendable. Several of my classmates were sent packing when they couldn't cut it. It behooved a trainee to strive to do his best, and not surprisingly, being one of the "good ol' boys" didn't hurt a smidgeon. Being a 'Tejano' (Texan) was a real asset.

Hooray! I had passed my 5 ½ written Immigration and Nationality Law and oral Spanish tests before reporting to the Academy - I seem to remember that the Service was without funds to send us to the Academy right away. Consequently, we took our "5 1/2s" at the station in December of 1961. We were fortunate in having a native speaker for Spanish and a very knowledgeable instructor otherwise. This outcome would have been much different if our in-service instructor had not been so qualified. Learning Spanish, obviously, was of primary importance. In fact, some crusty old border patrolmen even proffered the advice "to get a sleeping dictionary" to help with the learning process (surely they didn't think that one could learn Spanish by osmosis!). With the Academy training under our belts, April of 1962 left only several months before the last of our training at the station, and after completion of ten months of service and our long-anticipated final 10 month examinations, we all passed.

One could remain in the Patrol and be a journeyman officer his whole career, but advancing in the Service was not unlike any other ladder-promotion in other businesses. You had to keep your nose clean and progress in the normal scheme of things in order to seek advancement in the

While Patrolling Backwards

Service. I remember one area that was important was fingerprinting. Every instance in which a fingerprint was returned from the FBI because the prints were unreadable meant a gig. Some prints were because of the person's occupation causing blurred or obliterated friction ridges. Made no difference. If the prints were returned one got a gig! So, someone came up with the idea that if the prints would no doubt be returned, the officer did not use his real name, but signed the prints, "Herbie Swartz." as the fingerprinting officer. This bright idea took hold, but believe it or not, an officer by the name of Herbie Swartz was transferred into the station. It didn't take a rocket scientist to realize who got the award for having the most fingerprints returned.

I had the task of checking fingerprints one day. I had no fault with the actual prints, in fact they were easily classifiable. Since many of the 'campesinos' that we arrested were lacking in education and could not read or write, were told to sign their name with an X - "Ponga su equis en la linea," in English: put your X on the line. The officer who did the printing put "illiterate." under the X, but spelled illiterate wrong. Don't you think that this officer didn't get some ribbing about his literacy!

On July 9, 1962 my one year probation was over and we were considered journeyman officers. Now came the day-to-day application of what we had learned and acquisition of the skills and practical applications of the job which are attainable only by coaching and perseverance. There is an old expression "if you can't speak Spanish flawlessly, speak it fearlessly". An officer fresh out of the Academy was working the San Diego Greyhound Station in downtown San Diego one afternoon when he approached a well-endowed (portly, one might say), and well-dressed lady of Hispanic origin. She presented her Border Crossing Card (a Mexican visa.) Not trying to be too officious, and not knowing she was the wife of the Mexican Consulate he asked of her several questions in Spanish. One of the queries regarding her personal data was her birth date. This really set her off! Emboldened with the advice of speaking fearlessly and obviously not flawlessly, he asked, after looking at her card, "?Cuantos anos tiene usted? (How many asses do you have?) He simply wanted to know how old she was in order to match her verbal information with that of the card. The lady became unglued. She read him the riot act in Spanish - which he was obviously unable to readily translate. The Spanish word 'ano' means derriere. The middle letter in the Spanish word for "year" is actually a separate letter "n" which is pronounced n-yay instead of en. Maybe she wouldn't have been so hysterical if she had been svelte and hadn't been endowed with a humongous behind.

While Patrolling Backwards

In the early '60s the San Diego Greyhound Bus Station yielded as many apprehensions made at the Chula Vista Station. The crux of the operation was to identify and arrest any non-Americans traveling by bus who did not carry Border Crossing Cards, valid for visits to the U.S. of 72 hours duration or less and for travel no further than 300 miles from the border. Our task was to 'break' an alien into admitting a violation of this status, as well as to apprehend Mexican prostitutes and undocumented aliens.

One afternoon my partner and I were working the bus station and I realized that the majority of individuals with whom I spoke didn't understand English, so I thought to myself, what the heck, I'll use my Spanish to identify myself and question them. It worked well for a while, but then I was forced to change my tactics. Passengers started debarking from an arriving bus, and the very first one off and backing down the steps was one who appeared to be a likely apprehension. Then I started my spiel. "Soy official del Servicio de Imigracion". "Por favor, dejeme ver su documentos de Inmigracion". Translated, I told the gentleman that I was an officer of the Immigration Service, and I asked him in a polite manner to see his immigration papers. This guy turned around, and told me in plain English, and loud enough for everyone nearby to hear - "I don't speak your god-damned lingo." Bellicose would be putting it mildly to describe this guy. I was so embarrassed, I thought I would die! Lesson for the day: Don't start off with Spanish until you see their face!

While Patrolling Backwards

We didn't actually have an office per se in the bus station, but we had a write-up room upstairs which sufficed. My partner and I collared a Mexican prostitute who had apparently fallen through the immigration screening at the border. She looked the part, heavy makeup, gaudy dress, and most of all she carried a health card in her purse that is required of all prostitutes in Mexico. We took her upstairs for write-up - we always worked in pairs to avoid any semblance of impropriety. While I was asking her questions during the write-up, my partner was going through her belongings. He found a small flowered, zippered bag containing white power, at which time he asked me, "Hey, Hattery what does heroin taste like?" Before I could say anything, he gingerly wet his little finger in his mouth, then into the contents in the zippered bag, and announced he was going to call the office to find out. I looked up at our apprehension and asked her in Spanish "?Que tiene usted en la bolsa?" What's in the bag? Without any equivocation or hesitation, she answered 'douche powder' and made a waving motion at the lower part of her body. When my partner returned, shaking his head, I knew that he had not acquired the information that he was looking for; however, with a grin on my face, I quickly told him, "You've been licking douche powder." He made me swear that this news was between us only. I'm not completely sure if I've kept my promise or not.

The assignment at the bus depot was plain clothes, which meant either suit or sport coat and tie. We all stuck out like a sore thumb from the denizens of the bus station, and we were sometimes mistaken for Mormon missionaries. Fortunately, being decked out in our $5.00 used suits, many purchased from Jesse's (our favorite second-hand store) and raring to go, we were new to all the arriving and departing passengers on the buses.

The Border Crossing Card was quite important to its holders; as most citizens of Mexico were required to have a visa to visit the United States, this card served that purpose. One was obviously difficult to acquire, and a violation of its terms would leave one without a legal way to enter the United States for one year. Naturally, some holders were reluctant to admit to violations that would require its relinquishment. I am hesitant to apprise the reader of a mechanism we utilized but the creative methods used desire an expose. Someone had the idea of putting a black light in a cardboard box, with a peep hole in the top and places to put the detainee's hands into the box. The individual then was prepped about a "scientific" phenomenon: If an individual had been in the United States for more than 72 hours and drinking our water (remember, the cards were only

While Patrolling Backwards

valid for temporary visits of 72 hours or less), his or her fingernails would glow white when introduced to the inside of the lighted black-light box. Naturally, everyone's nails will glow under a black light. We were quite successful with this ruse. A majority of the time the alien would 'break' to the offense, offer no excuse, except to say "Pues, se quede in Los Estados Unidos no mas de siete dias", translated, "I am in the United States no more than seven days." As if that would rectify the situation. While a majority of the time the above referenced ruse worked, there were frequently poor ol' campesinos from south Mexico who lived so far in the boondocks they had never even seen a telephone. Their understanding of such a scientific principal as water and its reaction on one's nails was beyond their comprehension.

Apprehensions during the busiest months of summer numbered between 400 and 600 at Chula Vista. A good share of the total apprehensions made in a transportation check were for violations of status on border crossing cards. Reflecting back, it was a necessary job and the unfortunate Mexican were required to wait for one year to re-apply or do like thousands of others over the years: 'brincan la linea sin documentacion', cross the fence without documents.

Back in uniform and back on the line we were assigned to a unit, which included a supervisory officer and his "secundo" (second in command, usually an officer with a year's service under his belt) along with six to eight officers of varying degrees of knowledge and experience. The patrolling that we did was somewhat of a misnomer. Actually it entailed driving our 'rag-top' jeeps in compound low two or three miles an hour as we covered a designated specially dragged road paralleling the border, scrutinizing carefully, or more aptly put, 'sign-cutting' for evidence of a person's illegal entry. A popular attempted deception used by our friends from south of the border were to walk backwards across the road or to brush their tracks out with a handful of sage brush. This seldom worked. A pithy saying by one of our most adept 'sign cutters' once said during a national television onsite interview regarding our porous border, that such manners of covering one's illegal entry "stuck out like a diamond in a goat's ass". Part of his conversation was "bleeped" but I understood what he said - I had heard it before! Our sign-cutting roads, many of which carefully maintained with our contrived drags, were Rube Goldberg affairs made with ½ tractor tires or pieces of runway landing mats dragged behind our vehicles. Every shift began with dragging an assigned area sign cutting road so that we began with a "clear slate."

We had many characters at my assigned station, and it seemed that they were more prone to having to explain that they were involved in something

15

that went awry. Anything that involved government property definitely had to be explained fully in writing. In this vein, coming in early one morning before sunup, I noticed a fellow officer hunting and pecking his story out on a typewriter in the write-up area in the office, which in no small way piqued my curiosity, as he was assigned midnight to eight in the morning from the river bottom area to the beach, where he should have been. He let up on his typing long enough to tell me, upon being asked, "well, while patrolling in the river bottom I had a coughing fit, and coughed up a lung-hanger that inappropriately landed on my tie, the process of trying to wipe same from my tie, caused me to be distracted, causing me to crash into a parked pick-up truck." I am sure the Station Senior got a chuckle out of this story, and the officer no doubt received an appropriate admonishment.

Vehicle accidents were not uncommon at the station, mostly because of the terrain we had to negotiate with our 4-wheel drive jeeps and International Scouts. In fact for whatever reason or the other, accidents did happen but a full report would need to be accomplished addressed to the Station Senior, covering in full detail of everything surrounding the accident. One would be surprised how innovative an officer could be in describing a vehicle mishap. Usually if an officer did not make a habit of wrecking a government vehicle an oral admonishment sufficed. The particular written excuse that strikes me funny was the one that I perused, with the subject: "While Perusing Backwards ...." (by the way, my wife has heard this story several times over the years and it was her suggestion to use this as an apt title for the book). It involved the officer backing into a closely following moving civilian car on a back-country road while being enrapt in checking some tracks (sign). In second place would be the one where the officer was sign-cutting 3-4 miles an hour, in compound low when a large boulder in the road caused the vehicle to go end over end on a straight away.

We had our share of punsters, jokesters, and the like at the station. We were not always serious - one afternoon I was conversing with our radio operator (a retired Navy radioman)at the door of his radio room, who without doubt had been around in his career, and one would think it would be difficult to get anything past him. Down the hallway our beloved janitor was working his way towards us. The radioman was applying Chap Stick to his lips at the moment that the janitor got along side us. The operator said to him, "Hey, Ralph did you ever indulge in other than standard sex?" It was however, described to Ralph in a more profane and less delicate manner - language more appropriate to a sailor. (Many years later President Clinton indulged in this behavior with Monica Lowensky). Without slowing down with his broom, Ralph replied laconically, "Nope, it chaps my lips." Charley, the radioman, knew that he had been one-upped by the janitor, and with nary a riposte, humbly returned to his work without a comeback for Ralph.

Working the 8A to 4P shift on the line and rotating with my partner in the Tijuana river bottom one fine sunny morning (which we had plenty of), my partner radioed me asking for a meeting in the river bottom. The main street in Tijuana, Calle Revolucion, ends at the 4-strand barbed-wire fence separating the United States from Mexico. As I drove up not knowing what to expect, my partner was standing at his jeep and in the process of telling a male individual to not come any closer. The individual, standing casually, was at least 40 yards away and had been confronted by my partner just after the former had climbed over the fence. Not seeking to embarrass the man, he asked me quietly, "Did you get a whiff of him?" Sadly, it was determined that the fence jumper was quite unclean and disheveled, wearing well-worn sandals without socks, and appeared to not know where is was or how he got there. He acted like something serious was wrong with him. It turned out, that he had a small personal amount of marijuana on his person, that he was that he was smoking it to alleviate the pain that he was suffering. The smell emanating from him even at a distance made him reek to high heaven! The poor soul had exposed bones for toes - without a clinical diagnosis it was plain to see that he was suffering from leprosy. My partner tried to pawn him off on me to haul him to the station to be written up as an illegal. But I quickly disabused him of that idea and suggested that we forget that we had an apprehension. We finally ended up taking him and turning him over to Mexican Immigration, just a short distance away, so that Mexican Red Cross could take care of him. The word got out that Hattery and his partner apprehended a leper and a Service jeep was used to haul him in. For at least a month, and until the matter blew over, no one used the vehicle that was used to haul the leper.

Close to the same time-period, I was assigned to the river bottom and its environs on the graveyard shift. Just at daybreak, I was parked scanning the area when an individual disembarked from a taxi on the end of Calle Revolucion on the Mexican side of the border and quickly climbed the four-strand barbed-wire fence; I approached him just as he got to the United States side of the border. He was obviously shaken up and anxious to get out of Mexico, and he told me as much. He identified himself as a American-born citizen, and quickly explained that he had shot himself in the calf of his leg while trying to quell a disturbance in his bar that he owned some distance away. The way he was running belied this tale. According to his story, he was married to a Mexican citizen and some drunk "pachuco" types came into his bar and starting to tear the place up. In order to defend himself and to keep them from wrecking his place, he retrieved his .25 caliber semi-automatic from behind the bar and fired several rounds hitting the miscreants, but he didn't they think that they were severely wounded. In the ensuing melee one of his misplaced rounds found his left calf. He knew the Mexican cops would shoot him and ask questions later so he left his bar post haste! After a thorough interview it was indeed determined that he was a citizen of the United States.

November 22, 1963, just a few days past my youngest son's first birthday I was assigned to office duties when my wife called to tell me that President Kennedy was shot by an un-known assailant while in a motorcade in Dallas, Texas, early that morning. The word spread quickly at the station, and in a matter of what seemed like minutes all officers were alerted and called in to begin a 24-hour siege of the border area. Immediately, all traffic southbound into Tijuana was stopped, including automobile and commercial traffic. Extra patrols were initiated on the border to stop anyone trying to surreptitiously enter Mexico. It was unknown at this point whether or not there was an international conspiracy to kill the president, thus the border blockage. For some odd reason, freeway traffic southbound was negligible, and I had a first-hand look as since I was assigned to the freeway just north of the San Diego Police Checkpoint, about 200 yards north of the entrance into Mexico. Vehicle drivers were courteous and were understanding under the circumstances, when I advised them that Tijuana was temporality closed for the time being. By early afternoon, the situation remained at a standstill. At about 3:00 p.m., I caught a glimpse of what appeared to be a a line of 25 or 30 elementary school children on the sidewalk several hundred yards distant being lead, with a child in each hand, by Father Tulio, the local priest of the Catholic Church in San Ysidro, California. I saw that he was challenged by one of my colleagues, but he was detained only a short time when he proceeded on his way to Mexico. Speaking later with my colleague he said that the priest was adamant and would not take no for any answer, and was personally delivering his charges home.

In the late Spring or Summer of 1965 a mystery occurred the conclusion of which I am sure still lingers. The tracks of three illegal entrants were 'cut' on our sign-cutting road that paralleled the Mexican border and separated our two countries by four strands of barbed wire. This wire barrier was primarily in place for the purpose of keeping diseased cattle from crossing from Mexico. The crossing took place near the airport mesa, so named for the Mexican International Airport. Three or four of our permanent sign-cutters took up the chase, and worked that day until dark and recommenced the tracking the next day to well into the next late afternoon, following sign to the mountain range north and east of where the tracks started, a good 10 miles plus, when the trackers came upon a clearing in the brush that covered the mountain. What they came upon was almost indescribable: in their view lay the petrified remains of a woman, fully clothed, with a scarf over her face, seemingly to protect her face from the sun, wearing beaded moccasins that showed hardly any wear on the soles. It was undetermined how long she lay there, and how she died, but it must have been months. The tracks of the interlopers made a fast retreat back to Mexico. A Navy helicopter notified for to recover this unfortunate's corpse. San Diego ambulance was requested though our radio operator. After a thorough interview a determination was made that the individual was actually a citizen of this country.

Charlie the radio operator knew his job backwards and forwards. All day-time phone calls came through the radio room, therefore all in-comings were answered either by Charlie or his replacement. Charlie had the most solicitous, pleasant telephone and radio voice. It is hard to imagine anyone more pleasant or helpful in his job. One Sunday afternoon when assigned to headquarters and things were a bit slow my partner and I decided to test Charlie's helpfulness and patience. My partner had a perfect Old Country accent. With this accent he called Charley on an outside line. Charley answered the phone in his most mellifluous, courteous and helpful voice, at which time my partner spoke of going as a tourist to Tijuana and queried if it would be OK to take his dog with him. Cheerfully he was told by Charlie to enjoy his visit to Mexico and assured him that as long as he had a valid rabies certificate for his dog there would be no problem. We waited about one hour, then my partner called Charley back, and before Charley could finish his telephone repertoire the so-called Englishman asked him if he had been the one who had advised him about his dog, at which time he said yes. Before Charley could get another word out of his polite mouth, my partner, with his contrived English accent, said "You son of a bitch, they killed my dog!" There was a brief moment of silence on the other end of the phone, when Charley screamed back, "Don't call me a son of a bitch, come up here and say that." "I'm on my way up there," the Englishman replied, and hung up. It took us awhile to regain our composure and in doing so we headed around the corner of the office and down the hall to the radio room. Charley was pacing the floor in the waiting area, with his eyes fixed down the hill when we approached him. Having a difficult time maintaining our composure, we asked innocently and almost simultaneously, "What's going on?" Obviously in a snit which I had never previously observed, Charlie replied, "Some Limey bastard called me a son of a bitch on the phone and is on his way up here." We couldn't keep this to ourselves long, when almost soto voice in Charlie's ear, my partner cut into his English accent. It reminded me of the Coyote and Road Runner cartoon when the coyote slunk away with his ears almost trailing the ground after he had been had.

Just about everyone had the opportunity to be the butt of a practical joke at one time or another, and no one was immune, even yours truly: I was assigned to the processing unit in Sector Headquarters, mid-summer of 1965, just across the pavement from the Chula Vista Station, about 75 yards distant. We had the responsibility in the unit to check everyone one else's paper work, decide on prosecutions, prepare orders to show cause, warrants of arrest and conditions of release, read the charges in Spanish to our detainees and ultimately manifest all detainees on a daily basis by Service bus to Calexico, California, a main detention center. There they would be in custody for up to 2 weeks to await FBI checks. Getting to the point though; at about 6:00 a.m. one morning as I was engrossed in getting the paperwork ready for our daily load of detained aliens. I was aware of firecrackers being shot off behind my back, in the darkened morning, some distance from where I was out. Then, the most "gosh awful" sound interrupted my thoughts. Naturally, I turned around very quickly when the sound reached my ears, and I looked through my window, which had been broken, and glass from it blasted me in the back of my head. Two of my fellow officers had just booked in a "smuggling case" in the office across from me and had been shooting off confiscated firecrackers that they had obtained from the down at the port of entry.

Well, eventually they observed me hard at work and thought a fire cracker thrown in my direction would interrupt my reverie, not actually intending to cause any damage - just to scare me! There was a nicely manicured hedge outside my window, and the thinking was a well thrown M-80 would land on the hedge and go no farther. Wrong! Not only did the M-80 scare the daylights out of me, but it destroyed the window pane. The first thing that I saw, after turning around, and looking through the smoke and the broken window was my fellow officer shrugging his shoulders in disbelief. Naturally, I received apologies all around. A window repairman had to be called out to repair the damage before the powers to be came on duty. The duty assistant chief did show up and glanced at the repair truck as he drove to the parking lot. To help my so-called buddies out I intercepted the duty officer near the coffee shop we had at the back of the station, near the parking lot, and invited him for coffee. As we sat enjoying out coffee, for 30 minutes or so, the firecracker miscreants showed up in the coffee shop and signaled me surreptitiously that the window was fixed. To this day, one of the fellows whom I have known for nearly 50 years, says his partner threw the M-80. I am even getting to think that he was right, the other officer being the culprit. I am not sure how much they had to chip in for the window, but I think it was $25 each for that early Saturday morning call out by the repairman. Back in those days it was quite a chunk of change to shell out, especially in light of what our salary was. When I jibe my buddy about this he denies any implication, but does admit that I "saved their asses" that day!

While Patrolling Backwards

Immigration Inspector - Kennedy Airport

What is most difficult for me to relate is the fact that after arriving in New Jersey during Easter week of 1966 we lost our youngest son, Christopher Colman, 3 ½ years of age. Just the day after our arrival, on April 5, 1966, our son was struck by a car on busy Kinderkamack Road, in the quiet little borough of Montvale. For all practical purposes, Chris was killed instantly, but was on life support for two days. He was taken off life support and shortly thereafter he passed away - it was Good Friday. Without the support of our families, my family with whom we stayed while pending our move to Long Island, and all our friends, neighbors and co-workers in California we would would not have endured. It was months after moving to Long Island before I was able to even consider visiting in Montvale again. It has been nearly 45 years since we lost our son, who would be nearly 50 years of age now. A day does not go by without my thinking of him! His sister Melanie Ann was born in Jamaica, Long Island, New York on January 13, 1967, almost exactly nine months after he was killed. He is buried next to his grandparents in the serene, well-kept cemetery overlooking the Silver Valley, in Kellogg, Idaho.

My entry on duty in New York was comprised of an introduction at 20 West Broadway, New York City to the District Director, whose name now slips me, and my workplace boss, Robert E. Lee - nope, no relation to the Lee family of Virginia. I was given the option of staying in New York City and working as an adjudicator, with Sunday and holiday inspections duties at John F. Kennedy Airport (JFK). My option was full-time inspector at the airport. Strangely, when I met the District Director, he reminded me of the Wizard of Oz--not the fan-fare aspect, but possibly it was just his presence. He certainly did wield a lot of real power. The New York District Office at the time was probably the busiest and most important of the district offices in the country.

While Patrolling Backwards

Indoctrination as an immigration officer at John F. Kennedy International Airport involved shadowing experienced officers and learning the procedures and mechanics of the job. What impressed me the most was the wonderment of having to work in such fashion! There was an unwritten policy that no more than two minutes would be expended on each arriving passenger. Of course, arriving U.S. citizens were a 'slam dunk' but they comprised only a small fraction of the arrivals. Arriving aliens were another situation. Arriving at JFK were aliens from every country of the world, coming as visitors, students, exchange visitors, visitors for business and pleasure, diplomats, transits without visas, permanent residents, ad infinitum. They had with them passports from every country of the world and documentation that required close scrutiny in order to determine their admissibility. Clearly, the position required instant recall of facts relating to validity of passports, classes of non-immigrant aliens, excludability of aliens, immigrant visas, visitors for pleasure, visitors for business, and terms of admission. When the individual was found admissible his/her passport, arrival record and Customs Declaration was stamped with the date, place and period admission. A copy of the arrival/departure record was stapled in the passport and the duplicate was retained for control purposes by our Service. U.S. passports were stamped along with their Customs declaration.

Reflecting upon admission stamps, I remember an event that caused me such embarrassment I thought I would die! Our inspection booths had a counter about chest high. I had erroneously inked up my stamp with too much ink and upon stamping this particular lady's documents I sprayed her with ink across her blouse about countertop high. Of course, she was unaware of this; all she saw was what I had done to my newly-starched uniform shirt. She thought this was quite funny and was laughing out loud as she walked away. I didn't hear anything more about this but I have always wondered if her laughing turned to tears when she saw the mess on her blouse.

While Patrolling Backwards

In mid-summer we had throngs of arriving passengers that numbered over 30,000 and it was estimated that from the time a plane blocked and an individual had been checked by Public Health, U.S. Immigration and U.S. Customs it took a time span of about 3 hours. The cacophony of all these people in the waiting area, which must have been in the hundreds, was astounding! Usually there would be 3 or 4 planes blocking at a time and waiting for them were representatives of the various airlines to assist their customers with the needed documentation. An inspector did not have the time nor in some cases the inclination to complete needed arrival records for Immigration purposes. So one would hear shouts from the inspectors: Luftansa, Alitalia, BOAC, PanAm, Air France, Icelandic, Avianca, etc. mixed with the chorus of all the other noise, making it sound like the Wall Street Stock Market on its busiest day.

We mainly had two shift assignments: 7:00 a.m. to 3:00 p.m. or 1:00 p.m. to 9:00 pm. The early shift, 7:00 a.m. to 3:00 p.m. was the 'ball buster' for the simple reason that every day, particularly between May and September one would receive an early call at 2:30 a.m. or so to report within an hour to JFK to inspect an off-scheduled flight, then at 3:00 p.m. you would be advised by the day-shift supervisor that you were being held over to around 8:30 p.m. Seven days in a row were all that one could handle of this! Afternoon shift would come next for seven days, but without the onerous overtime.

I would have to say that the Icelandic flight that blocked around 7:30 a.m. nearly every morning was the most interesting. Icelandic was a turbo-prop plane and seldom if ever was it off schedule, thus incurring no overtime charges. It was the cheapest way to fly from Europe and it was always full to capacity - around 200 souls (soul was the nomenclature used by the airline industry to indicate passenger). The clientele was usually students or other people of lesser means. One might say that Icelandic could be described as the Greyhound Bus of the skies. Before they were famous I met and inspected Sonny and Cher Bono and Sonny's brother on Icelandic. To me they were just some more hippies traveling second-class.

Even though the days were quite hectic at JFK, it could not be said that the work was not interesting. Every day there was an abundance of celebrities of every ilk that we greeted, inspected and sent on their way. The JFK experience included the processing of many passengers of known stature: Jayne Mansfield (just a week before she was killed in a car wreck in Louisiana), Burt Lancaster, Montgomery Cliff (stoned out of his mind and his valet doing all the talking), Frank Sinatra (surrounded by his entourage. I was not impressed with his demeanor, standoffishness and self-importance), Diana Ross and the Supremes, Anthony Quinn (I remember him as particularly friendly. Had a large family group with him), Rock Hudson (I remember the contact representative saying she asked him about his leading ladies and he remarked "they don't like my garlic breath". It was some time later that he came out of the closet - boy, did that break my bubble. He had been one of my favorite actors, especially in Giant.), Marc Chagall (I didn't realize how famous he was until later), Sofia Loren and her husband Carlo Ponti (I didn't realize that she was so much taller than he). I was impressed by Charles A. Lindberg the most: When I was handed his passport, I right away knew who he was and I remarked to him, just to break the ice, they have an airfield named after you in San Diego. He looked at my name tag and replied, "Yes, Mr. Hattery, that goes back many years," and he continued to converse with me as if I were his equal. What a gentleman he was.

During the Christmas season of 1966 I also greeted by Morey Amsterdam, traveling with his wife and two children. He was on the Dick Van Dyke show about that time. It was one of my family's favorite. Anyway, his daughter who was about 8 or 9 years of age asked me what I was looking up in the book. Seeking to add a little levity to my inspection I told her I was working for Santa Claus and I was going to check it twice to be sure she had not been naughty but nice. It did not evince a even a small comment from her, and her father never cracked a smile. I wonder if their being Jewish had anything to do with their non-reaction?

To enhance my greeting skills I memorized a number of phrases in German, Italian, French, and I was at that time conversant in Spanish. I used these phrases sparingly because it encouraged persons to continue in their native tongue of which I knew not what they were saying. Anyway, way back in my line this busy summer day was an older couple from Iowa. In the interim before meeting the couple I utilized some of my foreign phrases. They were probably returning from their first trip to Europe and taking everything in. When they approached my booth, the gentleman said to me, "my goodness, how many languages do you speak?" And I replied, 'Spanish and broken English.' They left me with a smile on their face as I bade them adieu!

Later that summer, traffic just started to build up inside the inspection area when I noticed in a line to my left was a college professor I had had a number of years before and I motioned for him and I said, Mr. Priddy would you please come over here. He said to me, "My goodness, how do you know the names of all the arriving people?" I didn't let on right away that I had taken a speech class from him a number of years back. We exchanged pleasantries and he was on his way.

I always tried to be friendly and extend courtesies whenever possible. However I did drop from my greeting, "How was your trip?"; especially after a lady told me her husband had died over there, leaving me with only 'I'm sorry' and welcomed her back.

The spring and summer months were by far the busiest time at Kennedy Airport and in light of this we had extra help. Usually we had officers detailed from the District office but utilized seasonal help: students and teachers. Some were better than others, but on the whole we made do. On a summer afternoon in 1966, a seasonal officer was manning the booth next to mine. In the booth with him was a newly hired seasonal getting on-the-job training. I think they were friends and were in college together. Anyway, a black African diplomat, very distinguished looking, and his family with him appeared at the seasonal's booth. Keep in mind, that at that time Africa was in a state of turmoil and country boundaries were changing nearly every week. Mistakenly, the seasonal assumed that the diplomat's English was not good and that he did not understand when he was asked, "What was the number of the airline that you came in on?" Obviously attempting to impress his trainee, he stood up and spread his arms out in wing-fashion and asked him, "Which great iron bird did you come in on?" I thought to myself there is going to be hell to pay with that gaffe. Possibly an international incident? In a "huff" the diplomat declared in the Queen's best English, "We came in on Pan American 103." I was not privy to the outcome of this incident.

One late afternoon in September or October of 1966, three or four of us were relaxing in the crew booth between flights when a very regal-looking lady, dressed in finery and exuding wealth approached us and asked if it would be possible to go through to cargo and pick up her cat that she had had flown in. Anxious to help her, several officers chimed in and explained to her she was permitted to go through our area but she would need permission from public health to go on go through to the cargo area. After figuring that we were done with her, she reappeared shortly carrying a cage with a large fluffy white cat wearing what appeared to be a rhinestone necklace. The lady held up her prized animal and declared, "Would anyone like a cat?" Out of the mouth of the officer manning the crew booth came, "No, but I wouldn't mind a little pussy." The lady sucked in her breath, and exclaimed, "Well, I never...." as she fled away. Needless to say we all fled away as fast as we could, leaving only the officer who had made such a breach of etiquette. In my naivete I didn't realize it was alcohol talking - I found out later that the officer who made the faux pas was an alcoholic and had been drinking boiler makers, unbeknownst to the supervisor. If there had been a complaint filed I wasn't aware of it. Maybe she was a native New Yorker and was inured of the discourtesy of New Yorkers. The inebriated officer met his demise on his way home several years later when he was killed in a traffic accident.

Arriving to work early one morning in January of 1967 I was asked by an off-duty supervisor to inspect an Russian Aeroflot aircraft in another section of the airport, that was carrying Andre Gromyko (Minister of Foreign Affairs) and Alexei Kosygin (Chairman of Council of Ministers) that would be attending a United Nations special session. He said that he would accompany me and be available if any questions arose. At the site some distance from where arriving planes normally blocked was an airplane, the largest I had ever seen. It was a twin engine turboprop that I am sure was the pride of the Russian air fleet. It was well before the advent of the Boeing 747, but must have been almost as big. Standing just outside the door of the aircraft the foreign dignitaries were giving their obligatory speeches before a crowd of newsmen and politicos. At the conclusion of the arriving ceremonies my off-duty supervisor and myself boarded the plane.

The interior of the plane appeared to be the most colossal and well-appointed living room that up to that point, I had ever been. Before us was a beautiful solid ebony or mahogany round table, upon which were all the Russian passports; probably at least fifteen. In the center of this was a large teakwood bowl filled with fruit, mostly with sweet cherries. As we sat down, the Russian liaison officer shook hands with me and reintroduced himself to my boss, whom he had met on a previous occasion. I promptly got down to business inspecting the official passports, which held visas of high government authority.

At the conclusion of my inspection bottles of vodka and cognac were brought out along with what I assumed was expensive caviar. Drinks were poured all around. I don't think I mentioned but there were at least one dozen trench-coated (spy clothes?) men that partook of the festivities. Water glasses filled with vodka were first and toasts to President Johnson and Gromynko were in order. Of course I pretended that I was drinking. No one seemed to notice. I didn't drink much anytime and certainly not vodka or cognac that early in the morning. These toasts went on for some time and I could see that my supervisor was becoming quite affected (i.e., drunk).

My supervisor, looking at his acquaintance the Russian liaison officer and exclaimed to him in somewhat of an inebriated condition, "Where did you get those cherries?" referring to the bowl on the table. The Russian said "Ve get them in Russia" at which my supervisor exclaimed, "Bullshit. You don't get cherries in Moscow in the winter-time." "Ve learn to grow them in Russia in the vinter-time," he vehemently replied. At that, we picked up our stuff, thanked everyone for their courtesy and started for the door of this gigantic plane. Whew, I thought it was all over, when my supervisor stuck his head back in the door and yelled out, "I still think it's a bunch of bullshit about those cherries."

Working afternoon shift in 1967 and arriving my usual one hour early and getting out of my car, I viewed a late-model expensive car not far from where I had parked. In fact, it had been the second day that I had seen this vehicle, with all four tires flat, taking up valuable parking space. Not being in a very good mood, I was going to give the Port Authority a piece of my mind about their reluctance in removing disabled cars from the lot and freeing up valuable parking space. Being occupied with other matters, letting the matter slip, I didn't make the call to the Port Authority. I was reminded the very next day of the disabled card incident: emblazoned across the front page of the "New York News" picture newspaper was the same car that I had walked past two days in a row. "Body of adult male, trussed up and murdered was found in trunk of late-model luxury car trunk at JFK I've always wondered if that could have been some of John Gottis' (New York crime boss+ work. Apparently some concerned employee did place a call to the Port Authority.

About the middle of June 1967 we got word at Kennedy Airport that two of our fellow officers: Theodore L. Newton, Jr. and George F. Azrak, young officers working at Temecula, California, an outstation of Chula Vista Sector, on traffic check were killed by marijuana smugglers in the wee hours of the morning of that fateful day. This had a two-fold effect on me. Just the horrific nature of this crime bothered me, but I shudder to think it could have been me and my partner. I was thinking of the old expression, "only by the grace of God, go I."

Just before departing to my first promotion as an immigration inspector at Kennedy Airport, the latter part of March, 1966, with another Border Patrol officer were assigned line watch on midnight to 8:00 a.m. near the border station of Tecate, California. Sitting in our Plymouth sedan, lights off, engine idling on a dark and lonely. road running perpendicular to the border road. Since the port closed at midnight, any traffic from that direction would have entered the United States without inspection; the border was around 5 miles from us.

My partner and I conversing quietly in the vehicle, not really thinking about the dangers of the job, at the same time spotted a vehicle rounding the curve on the crooked paved road from the direction of the closed port.

Keeping the car lights off, I released the emergency brake, put the vehicle in drive, slowly coasting to intercept the on-coming vehicle, and alert to what may happen next! Turning the car lights on as we approached the other vehicle and were pleasantly surprised, and I am sure, relieved, appeared a deputy sheriff vehicle with light bar and the whole schmeer. We waved to each other in passing.

It is doubtful, but not beyond the realm of possibility, even though collectively we had nearly 25 years experience (me with big 5 years) we could have had the same thing happen to us that happened to Officers Newton and Azrak. (Google Newton/Azrak for the full story.)

At Journeyman School a number of years after the notorious killings I met a contemporary of mine, whom I worked with at Chula Vista in the Border Patrol. He had been part of the manhunt (one of the largest manhunts ever launched in the State of California. It was recounted to me that it only took 2 days when the Border Patrol vehicle was found, covered with brush next to to an old dilapidated prospector's cabin. Inside the cabin through the open door could be easily seen the two patrolmen hand-cuffed around an old pot-bellied stove. Looking up the hill at the cabin he said that he had seen enough and went no further. Choking up somewhat, he said that was the first time that he had seen grown men cry!

As the busy summer of 1967 at Kennedy Airport came to a halt - in fact my last day as an inspector was Labor Day, my days and unequivocally the most interesting days that I would encounter in the next 7 years in Inspections was coming to a halt, and leaving behind me were experiences, incidents, co-workers, and people would be forever ingrained in my consciousness.

Here we go again! We were now Montana bound after being selected for reassignment to the northeastern port of entry of Morgan, Montana, named after some pioneer who had made a contribution to history in that part of the State.

While Patrolling Backwards

Immigration Inspector - Morgan, Montana

My wife, son and daughter left New York via airplane on September 1, 1967 en route to north Idaho to visit folks before coming to Montana. I left New York in a new 1967 Chevrolet Impala which we purchased just before our departure. It was the first new car that we had ever owned and we were extraordinarily proud and protective of it. My cross country trip took two full days to southeastern Montana, spending three days in motels along the way.

Our new home was about 150 miles due north where I had spent my last night. I found it necessary to vet my new duty assignment of Morgan, Montana so that I would have something to describe to my wife. Our new home would be 55 miles north on highway 191 of Malta, Montana. I had never seen a road sign like this at any place that we had lived: "Pavement Ends 10 Miles." Having just left Malta, Montana, I headed up Highway 543 (now Montana highway 191), destined to Morgan, Montana, 50 odd miles north of Highway number 2 at Malta.

After about the first 10 miles the countryside was beautiful, open undulating prairie land, sparsely treed, with mostly scrub brush. It was the middle of September 1967, and most of the greenery had turned to light golden. But just like the advertising says 'the big sky country' I was able to see why. Just after the first 10 miles had gone, the sign appeared. Knowing for sure that could not be right; for heaven's sake, the paved road couldn't disappear! Then 'ka-thump' our 1967 Chevrolet Impala car that had just been purchased in New York brand new, which was our proud possession, drove off the pavement and on to the worst-maintained, purportedly gravel road, that I have ever been on - and I have been on some logging roads and sign cutting roads that would put this road to shame!

I slowed down to a crawl, just cringing while rocks and gravel hit the underside of the car. This so-called road continued on for another 35 miles after the "Pavement Ends 10 Miles" sign. In the distance appeared a railroad, several silos, a run-down, dilapidated old store, a bar (beer joint), the remnants of an old hotel and a very small post office with a flag pole flying the U.S. flag. This so-called oasis or wide place in the road was called Loring, Montana. I still had 17 more miles to go before reaching our destination at the Port-of-Entry of Morgan, Montana. The Canadian port across from our port was Monchy, Saskatchewan.

Up the hill from Loring, Montana I continued on my way, crossing White Water Creek, several miles up the road. Surrounded by dried prairie grass and brushy hilly country I could see, looming ahead, the Port with two identical residences almost side by side. The office had on the north side a Russian olive shelter-belt with trees that were 10 - 15 feet high. Between the office and the shelter belt was a large flag pole, flying Old Glory. The Port had a large two-part aluminum gate. During business hours the gate was opened with ½ opened on each side of the highway. When the gate was closed, both halves were brought together and chain-locked. Each gate half-gate had a stop sign.

It so happened that our home would be the house nearest the office, all of 25 yards away. The homes were commodious, with ranch-style brick façades and three bedrooms. Each home as well as the office had emergency generators, and because the land did not 'perk,' our sewer system was comprised of two large septic tanks. It was called a NoDak Sewer System. A huge gravel pile, at least 100 feet long and at least 50 wide was about 50 yards from the homes in which the water overflow from the septic tanks was pumped by submersible pump. Our water well was about 10 feet deep and heated night and day, as needed. The gravel, I found out, had to be trucked from more than 100 miles away.

Another distinctive feature at the port was the 65 foot transmitting/receiving tower just behind the office. We had two channels on our border patrol radio and due to the unobstructed transmission we had, there was hardly a place in the part of Montana north of highway 2 from North Dakota to Idaho that we couldn't reach on channel 2. The ports 50 miles to the west and to the east were easily reachable on channel 1. On top of the tower we had a television antenna with which we were able to get several snowy stations, which we relished because it was all we had! The only drawback to the radio and instant communication with the other ports of entry and the Border Patrol operator in Havre, Montana was that we picked up audio transmissions on our personal television. Fortunately, our night-time television was not affected.

The inspector whom I was to relieve glad-handed me when I drove up. He had a smile on his face and apparently he had been anticipating my arrival. He showed me around the place and introduced me to the Customs officer with whom I would be working and his family. From what I had gathered, he either could not get a transfer or he figured that owning a service station in Oklahoma, where he was originally from, was his best life's endeavor. In any case, he was out of there. He felt it important that my indoctrination should take several hours, and I could stay in the relief quarters in the office. The surrounding area was certainly disappointing, to say the least. In a hurry to catch up with my family in north Idaho, I made an excuse that needed my presence, so I thanked him and told him that I would see him in two weeks.

I drove straight through from Morgan to Kellogg, Idaho (over 400 miles) where my family was staying. I put off explaining in detail to my wife with her endless questions, what our new duty assignment was like. I just told her, 'just wait and you'll see'. In two short weeks, my holidays were over and my wife and two children and myself headed to our new home in the high plains country of northeastern Montana. Leaving Idaho we took a cut-off at Missoula, Montana and eventually ended up on Highway 2, locally called the highline. Wending our way through some of the most spectacular scenery, high mountains from the western part of Montana we motored on highway 2. The western part of highway 2 covers "Going to the Sun Road", through Glacier Park.

As we continued eastward from there the country flattened out and the Browning Indian Reservation was our next destination. At least for ten miles on both sides of the Reservation we noticed small crosses, sometimes as many as four in a group usually near small bridges that dotted the highway, sometimes on straight stretches of the highway. We came to learn that fatal automobile accidents had occurred at these places. Montana, as far as I know is the only state that memorializes fatal car accidents in this way. Most of these are on Native American land where alcoholism and driving is a problem.

My contemporaries at Kennedy Airport, especially the New York born and bred couldn't even envision anyone leaving New York, especially a place like the hinterlands of Montana. I was almost beginning to believe them. After already having described my trip from Malta, Montana we arrived just ahead of the moving van and we were home for the next three years! The children appeared to be happy in their new environs, and the Customs family of three children and two adults made the transfer a lot more tenable for them. My wife, eminently endowed with common sense and practicality didn't exhibit any negativity that I recall, but just dug in to do her part to make a happy home for us! We would need to bide our time there for at least two years.

The family that we were replacing were busy in the process of loading their household effects in a large truck, in short order were off and running to their old home in Oklahoma. By the way, a number of years later, the officer whom I relieved found working on the 'outside' was not 'a bed of roses' and he rejoined the ranks of the Immigration Service, subsequently retiring from same. I'll bet he didn't come back to a small border port like Morgan. The pleasure on their faces said everything! They had been at Morgan for no more than two years and were more than ready to leave.

Traffic-wise, one could say that we went from the ridiculous to the sublime. Instead of 30,000 arrivals at Kennedy on a busy summer day I was to learn we didn't have that many arrivals in six months time! Winter-time traffic would get down to sometimes as few as one automobile a day.

Our summer port hours were 13 hours: 8:00 in the morning to 9:00 at night. We had arrived during the winter hours: 9:00 in the morning to 6:00 at night. We had as few as one car per shift to possibly ten cars, and in the summer we could have as many as 25 autos. Most of our traffic was local Canadian, with a few returning U.S. citizens. Due to the paucity of traffic we kept statistics on every arrival: License number, make, model year, passengers, destination.

There was only one time during my tenure at Morgan that we locked the highway gate during normal working hours. My co-worker could never recall it happening. One afternoon in early summer of 1978 I received word that the Canadian-Chinese family who lived in Val Marie, Saskatchewan, about 25 miles up the road from the port and who ran the restaurant there, had just come back from a visit to China at a place where there had been a cholera outbreak. I called the district office in Helena at which time I was advised to close and lock the highway gate until further notice. In about two hours time I was advised to resume normal operations and open the gate. If I recall correctly we didn't incur a big traffic back-up.

Obviously, one would wonder how an inspector would not go crazy in a place like this. I was blessed with what was called 'stand-by' paper work. To fill in my time, the Chicago district office furnished me adjudications work: extensions of stay, student transfers, exchange visitors, et cetera. From the Omaha district office I did all the immigrant arrivals for Nebraska and Iowa; that is, I prepared the Alien Registration Cards, addressed the relating envelopes, prepared Occupation Index Cards, and sent everything back to our Regional Office in Saint Paul, Minnesota for the lamination of the alien cards and mailing same to the new immigrants. Also, in February or March I alphabetized the Forms I-53 (aliens are required to report their residence in January, or 30 days after their arrival back in the U. S. every year) for all aliens residing in Iowa, Nebraska and Montana.

Along with all the adjudications work that I accomplished, I also completed all the In-Service Training Courses (14 in all) for the second time. I already had a certificate exemplifying my accomplishment in 1964.

What made this transfer notable, was having such a great partner, Allan Ganter, representing U.S. Customs, and of course our Canadian counterpart, Dick Faber, and his family, just across the street (in Canada), and his replacement, Tom Martin and his family, from Montreal, Canada. Almost all of our friends that we made are gone, with the exception of Tony Andre who farms and ranches just north of us in Saskatchewan. One family that is hard to forget who lived just ¾ of a mile up the road in Canada was the Davis family. They so much reminded me of Percy Kilbride and Marjorie Main in the Ma and Pa Kettle movies I saw as a kid. Their old dilapidated farmstead and the junkie yard with the matching house was certainly reminiscent of them. Ralph Davis, the old man, had the habit of visiting the office at times and never bothered to worry about his manure- encrusted boots tracking up the floor from the front door to the counter.

The two Border Patrolmen in Malta, Montana, Lee Thomas and Jim Maxie became good friends, as well as Eric Green, a Mountie from Val Marie, Saskatchewan (about 25 miles up the road). Regular visitors to our office were the Mounties from Swift Current, Canada and Montana Fish and Game Agents, to name a few of our 'coffee customers.'

Just down the road south from us, about 3 miles lived the Scheffelmeir family. We saw Ray Scheffelmeir on a regular basis. We considered them friends and like all our friends they were there to help at any time. Eight years after we transferred from Morgan we received the distressing news that Ray and his wife, Dorothy along with a customer were murdered on November 8, 1978 in the Loring Bar that they managed or leased. What a shock it was to us! While we lived just north of there, 17 miles, years during which we were so complacent and felt so safe, never thinking something like that could happen. At the time neither Customs or Immigration officers carried a weapon on duty.

It seemed we never lacked for company. In the winter a regular visitor for dinner was the parish priest, Father John Foley, from Masefield, Saskatchewan. He enjoyed our pool table and shuffle board and used to spend hours at our house, his home away from home. He certainly was not shy, and liked to tell a joke, even if we had heard it many times before. One evening Father showed up and when he came through the door he took off his boots and placed his pork-pie hat on top of them, then asked me, "Andy, what does this remind you of?" I replied, 'you got me, what is it?' "It's an immigration inspector with all the crap kicked out of him." The joke was on me, of course, and elicited a big laugh from us all. He was only in his 40s so forgetfulness was not his problem, but he did wear that joke into the ground and told the same joke at different times on his visits. But, I finally got back at him! I told Ganter, my co-partner at the port father

Foley's joke. One evening father made his usual visit to our house, and for some reason we had gotten invited out. Father proceeded next door to the Ganter household and pulled the same joke on Ganter as he had done to me several times- not knowing that Ganter was on to him. When Father queried my partner, his reply had a different twist on it. He said that the pork pie hat resting on father's boots reminded him "of a Catholic priest with all the crap kicked out of him." That particular joke didn't make the rounds anymore.

Fortunately for us, we arrived at Morgan in early October, which gave us time to become acclimated to the on-coming winter weather. New York was cold and we had lots of snow. Montana weather in the winter is unlike any place we had ever been. It's hard to believe there was a two-week period our first winter that the temperature never got above 20 degrees below zero and several days were 50 below zero. Through a space in our picture window that had not frosted over, I remember looking at the outside thermometer with no mercury showing and thinking to myself the need for a new one on my next trip to Malta.

We were briefed on what to do and what not to do to battle the extreme winter weather, and the terrifically bad road between here and Malta, by my partner-to-be, Al Ganter: first and foremost I needed to get a tank heater installed on the heater hose of my car that would keep hot water circulating through the engine block when the car was plugged in and garaged. Secondly, I needed to protect the gas tank of my car by having a mechanic lower the straps holding the gas tank and place used belting in place to protect the front and bottom of the tank. As an aside, Al said that when cold weather did arrive not to fret about the running parked cars- people did this if they were unable to plug their auto in so their vehicles would not freeze up. We had emergency generators in both houses and the office, he said, so don't be alarmed when they automatically go on every Sunday morning at a fixed time, for a short while for testing. We had company from out of town several times and the generators went on before we could warn them, which of course, scared them out of their wits!

Winter, spring, summer and fall the wind blew. It was beautiful around there spring, summer and fall. The good thing about the wind was that if it blew during the day it would be quiet at night. It seemed the wind moderated the summer heat, making it comfortable; however, one could be flash-frozen in a short while in winter if extreme cold was introduced by wind and you were not dressed for it. Which reminds me of two stories:

A local rancher recalled to me that he had cattle on the open range near the port. And one wind blowing 20 degrees below winter day when he had brought molasses cake to the cattle that were in a draw near Smith's coulee

While Patrolling Backwards

west of the port. He left his pickup running facing into the wind while he delivered the important molasses cake that was needed by the cattle to maintain their body heat. He found his truck froze up upon his return.

When the wind settled down in the warm weather months the place was idyllic. At night the only noise would be the coyotes howling and in fall and early winter Canada and snow geese by the hundreds would resting while laying over and would feed on the harvested grain fields with their honking by the hundreds, within earshot of the port.

On one of Father Foley's evening visits he said that just that morning as he was looking out his parish residence window he saw a strange sight: just across his road he saw several people on the front porch of a old run-down house, remnants of a small village many years before. They were spreading a sheet out on the porch and the first thing that he thought was "What a day to have a picnic." Gathering his senses, he inquired and found out that the deceased, an old man who lived there who had been drinking (possibly ½ gallon of wine), had gone outside to go to the bathroom; he passed out on the porch and was flash-frozen where he fell.

The winter before we arrived at Morgan a young married woman from Climax, Saskatchewan was found frozen to death about ½ mile north of the port of entry at Turner, Montana (30 miles as the crow flies from Morgan). The nearest house in Canada was nearly 1 mile away. The story told to me by one of the Border Patrolmen that assisted in the search for her was that she had an American boyfriend. She would drive down from Canada and he would drive from the little town of Turner, Montana. They would meet along the border about a mile from the port of entry. That evening there was a blizzard with minus 20 degree temperatures. She arrived at their trysting spot but he did not because of the weather and not having a manner in which to contact her. She apparently got out of her car and started walking towards the nearest yard light -at least a mile away. She was not dressed properly for the weather and wore just regular shoes. The search party found her frozen remains on the lonesome windswept prairie where she had fallen.

Our son Jamie's school was twenty-five miles south and east of the port. He started at the Whitewater school in the 2nd grade. In the winter time the school bus came to the port and picked up him and the three Ganter children; it was dark when the bus came, and dark when the kids were delivered back home at night, making for a long day for them. This was ranch country and many of the boys at school wore cowboy boots. Jamie wouldn't indulge in the cowboy boots but did wear his favorite lace-up engineer boots. One of the things some of the other kids participated in was 4H-and he joined that when he was barely 10 years of age. He wasn't in for raising anything as a project but he gave a presentation on the major parts of the human body and won a blue ribbon for that. The judges were in wonderment how he knew so much about the human body. They thought him quite precocious for his age. Of course, his parents were proud of his accomplishment.

During Jamie's second year at Whitewater he contracted mononucleosis and was out of school somewhat for that. To show how accommodating the school principal was, on several occasions he flew up in his private plane to our grassy landing strip at the port to bring Jamie up to speed on his schoolwork so that he wouldn't get behind. It showed us a lot of concern on the part of the superintendent.

Loring, Montana was somewhat of a required way-stop at the bar which was the mainstay of this hole-in-the-wall place. Either on my way to Malta or my return trip I would stop in and gab with Maxine who bartended and have a Coke. One day, on an extremely cold day (probably at least 30 below zero), I pulled up, parked and noticed that behind the outside of the bar was a 1000 gallon propane tank with a fire underneath it. This was before we had conquered the moon and walked on its surface. As I walked in I asked Maxine why the fire under the propane tank - and duh! Wasn't that dangerous? She informed me that more than once they had done this because propane would not vaporize at extreme cold temperatures, particularly if the tank was less than ½ full, which was the case then. She said that the propane man was due anytime. She didn't seem to mind when I told her that it was my estimation that the whole works would be going to the moon! That day I didn't hang around there long. I don't think I stopped again when i saw them melting propane

While Patrolling Backwards

Our district office was in Helena, Montana, nearly 300 miles south and west of Morgan. It lay in a mountain valley that more often than not was called 'a banana belt.' When we were experiencing extremely cold temperatures on the border, the temperature would be 20 or 30 degrees warmer. I met the district director just once during my stay on the border when he and several Regional dignitaries came on an inspection trip in the early fall of 1970. The trips to the border stations made by the Deputy District Director John Reddy were as regular as clock work. Every six months, we would be given a heads up to advise us of his pending trip, which started on the border of North Dakota and during which he visited every station across Montana. He usually got to Morgan just in time for dinner, so we got to know him quite well. He would make a cursory check of the office and off he would go till his next trip. The Customs big-shots from Great Falls, Montana always made their trips unannounced.

I was very fortunate to have a co-worker like Al Ganter. He had been around a long time, in fact he spent the brunt of his career, over 25 years, at Morgan. He must have seen at least six to eight Immigration officers and their families come and go. On many occasions in the summer when he had the weekend duty he would be cooking in his driveway and wave for our 'customers' to come on down for lunch with him and his family. On more than one occasion I would have applicants query where the nearest gas-station was, and he would tell them to help themselves to his gasoline at his garage-he refused to take money and just explained to them to help someone in need when they had the chance.

One fall afternoon in 1968 a young American couple headed for Alaska were refused entry into Canada at Monchy, Saskatchewan for lack of funds. They subsequently returned to my office in an old clunker of a car with all their earthly belongings stashed all over the car. I sent them on their way, and Al Ganter, returning from Malta, noticed a car in the barrow pit just south of the port. When Ganter got to the port I told him about a young couple having been turned around an hour or so before. "I think they are off the road in their car, several miles from here. Let's go get them," he said. No sooner said than done. Sure enough, it was them. We towed their car with Al's truck and brought them back to the Ganter residence where they were put up and treated like long-lost relatives. I have long since forgotten their names, but we referred to them as 'Balmy and Clod.' They were in residence for about 2 weeks at the Ganters' residence and had just about taken over the place. Ganter made it known to me that it looked like they were going to stay permanently and their presence was getting to wear on his family, particularly in light of the fact that 'Clod' was starting to dismantle his car in their front yard. So Ganter used his connections and got "Clod" a grease-monkey job at a garage in Malta. We gathered up all 'Balmy and Clod's' personal belongings and towed them and their car to the Great Northern Hotel in Malta. We vouched for a night's lodging and we never saw them again, this incident didn't change Ganter's "good-guy" attitude, however.

Our port of entry included a pasture-like dirt airstrip about ¼ mile west of the office. Horses and cattle grazed on the strip and very occasionally when an aircraft did arrive, the pilot would make a low, slow fly over in order to alert us and more importantly to scatter the critters grazing there. One day, I processed the pilot and checked his small aircraft, a dual engine with retractable landing gear, and permitted him to go. His destination was Whitewater, Montana, south and east of Morgan about 25 miles. About a week after the aircraft arrival a gentleman driving a large flat-bed truck showed up for inspection. I recognized the man as the pilot of the preceding aircraft, and asked his purpose of entry. I could see that he was quite embarrassed in relating to me that after he had left the port a week ago that he proceeded to Whitewater, Montana. As he was landing he cut his speed on final nose-up approach to the prairie airfield there, and with the stall-speed indicator klaxon blaring, he landed with the gear-up! I never bothered to ask him how many air miles he had racked up or how long he had been flying. Later on that day I saw his truck loaded with his crashed airplane going through Canada customs. He could have been killed that day. He said he heard the stall speed indicator but must have been daydreaming.

All that a law enforcement officer had to do was to give us a call for information about an arrival that may have come through Morgan. Which brings me to a call I received one day from a Mountie in Swift Current, Saskatchewan, Canada. It seems that a young U.S. citizen male and his companion were stopped by the caller, near the trans-Canada highway, some distance from Morgan. I was able to verify that they had come through our port headed for highway 2 and Glacier Park. When stopped, the pair had a personal amount of marijuana in possession for which they were fined $100. The 'kicker' to this is that one Mountie thought that the other officer had collected the money before they were sent on their way. The Mountie obviously thought that he didn't have anything to lose by asking me to call the Border Patrol radio operator in Havre, Montana to see if a Border Patrolman could stop the miscreants and get the $100 fine that had been levied against them. I gave the Mountie the telephone number of Havre Border Patrol for him to call. No way could I stretch our liaison that far!

I was able to assist on this one Border Patrolman Lee Thompson from Malta, Montana, called to tell me that two Canadian gentlemen had just left Malta after carousing around the weekend. They had trashed their room at the Great Northern Hotel to the extent of $400 or $500. He said that they should be arriving at Canada Customs within the hour and gave me a description of their vehicle. Within 30 minutes or so I saw their vehicle go north and park at the Customs office. I walked over to the Canadian office and asked the gentlemen if they would come over to my office when they were finished. And there they came! I told them, "I heard you guys had quite a time in Malta over the weekend. " They were both in agreement- they had. To get to the point, I told them, "You guys are persona non grata in Malta unless you fork over the money to pay for the damage you did to your room. " In that part of the country, drinking and carousing
was their only entertainment. They looked at each other, reached in their pockets and each came up with around $250. I called the Border Patrol to retrieve the money to pay the hotel owner. Thus they retained their entertainment privileges south of the border.

In about November 1969, the Customs officer transferred out of the Turner, Montana station to Alaska. The Immigration officer had gotten on the bad side of our superiors in Helena and could not get a decent evaluation. So, he applied for and obtained the Customs job in Turner which left the port without an Immigration officer. Consequently, I came into the picture. By the way, within several months, he received a promotion to Customs Agent and left Montana. For six months I was unable to take a day off: On my weekend off at Morgan I relieved at Turner. Usually things were at least as slow as Morgan, with the usual Hutterites on their shopping trips or native Americans crossing the border.

One day, when things couldn't get any slower at Turner, a Mountie black and white police car pulled up with two officers in dress uniform and a hand-cuffed male in the back seat. The driver came into the office and explained that the American arrestee tore up the beer joint in Climax causing considerable damage, which he had done previously more than once. I glanced out the door just as the Mountie, sitting in the passenger side of the vehicle, was kicked in the head by the guy in back so hard that if he had not been wearing his Smokey Bear hat he would have cracked the windshield with his head. I called several local numbers and the only one person who wanted anything to do with him was his brother. The Mounties brought the drunk into the office. The guy was still in a belligerent mood and he kicked so hard at one of them he did a flip on his head, temporarily knocking himself out. The Mounties left as soon as this guy's brother vouched for him and took him away. It was destined that this drunk

While Patrolling Backwards

American would never again go on a bar rampage again. Just a few weeks later he was piloting his private airplane when he flew it into a coulee. It was never known whether he committed suicide or his plane had engine failure.

Seldom did any excitement occur at the border. It it was a big deal when our government veterinarian would make a regular appearance to inspect south-bound cattle utilizing the loading pens and scales across the road. Also, for several summers a touring carnival with dozens of concessionaires and workers would utilize the Canadian port of Monchy for their Canadian tour. Vehicles, rides, trucks and other paraphernalia would be backed up out of sight. The U.S. Customs officers' children would sell Kool-Aid and sandwiches to all comers. Usually, the whole process would take all day, until closing time of 9:00 p.m.

One afternoon, I was passing the time in the Canada Customs office and 'shooting the breeze'. Customarily, either the Canada Customs inspector visited us or vice versa several times a day. Dick Faber, the Canadian Customs officer looked south down the road, and remarked to me, "What's going on?" Now Dick had been there for years and had seen just about everything you could see in such a podunk place. Catching my eye, and for as far as I could see were U.S. Military trucks of every sort, caissons and cannons, jeeps, et cetera, the convoy wending itself northward to Canada. To get a rise out of Dick, with a smile on my face and a twinkling of my eyes. I said, 'Oh, I forgot to tell you, Dick you're working for me now." The look on Dick's face was: surely he must be jesting! It wasn't long until we found out that the procession was the U.S. Army en route to summer training in Canada.

Along with 27 other immigrations officers from Immigration offices across the United States, I was selected to attend session 14 of the Journeyman Immigrant Inspector Training Course at Glynco, Georgia from April 28 to May 14, 1970. Weather in Morgan, Montana had not yet settled down so it was a blessing to have such beautiful weather in south Texas to enjoy. That part of the U.S. is noted for this citrus fruit which thrives in this semi-tropical climate. Our training was a refresher-course in nature, covering most of our tasks as inspectors: Public Relations, Inspection of Aliens, Handling complaints, Intelligence, Exclusion and Deportation of Aliens, Acquisition of U.S. Citizenship through Naturalization, Derivation of U.S. Citizenship, Creation of Record, Acquisition of Permanent Residence through Employment and Family, Immigrant Visa Issuance Priority System, Admission of Aliens and Non-Immigrant categories and Immigrant categories.

While Patrolling Backwards

We had a presenter, Earl F. Titcomb, an associate commissioner in the Southern Region who covered several topics with us including public relations and inspections of aliens. The other instructors I have long since forgotten. He told us, "excuse the grammar, but always remember this: LOOK GOOD, TALK NICE, AND USE GOOD JUDGMENT." I have always tried to abide by this axiom and as the opportunity has arisen in the ensuing years, to pass it along. His admonishment to us was that in many instances we are the 'ambassadors' of the United States and the first impression people get when arriving here. Our comportment should be exemplary.

The designation, 'hard-ship' station has long since gone out of vogue, unless the inspection station at Presidio, Texas as still noted as same. However, most of the ports in Montana, and I suspect, in North Dakota and Minnesota, are difficult to fill and if at all possible, management likes to fill vacancies in such places with families. The port of entry at Presidio, Texas is the great-bend area Texas, over 100 miles distant from any town of any size. Maybe a port like Morgan, Montana being 55 miles from town; 35 miles of which were the worst road imaginable was just not far enough away! We certainly did not have adequate fire and police protection, sidewalks, doctors, hospitals, dentists, library, stores and other accoutrements of city life.

Management, knowing the nature of these out-of-the-way places, understands and is sympathetic when an officer is desirous of moving on. As an example of this: Mr. Reddy, our deputy district director, called me early one day in May of 1970. He told me he had the resignation on his desk of an officer at the East Port, Idaho port of entry just north of Sand Point, Idaho, and that as soon as possible I should request a transfer there. Without any hesitation I prepared the request, and since it was not mail day (we received mail delivery Monday, Wednesday and Friday), I delivered my request in person to the post office in Malta, Montana, 55 miles distant, one way.

A month or so later I had not received a response about my request, so I called the district director and asked him if the East Port, Idaho position had been filled. He told me I came in a close second for the job, but he was so impressed that the officer who had beat me out took a demotion from an examiner position in Los Angeles. Of course, I knew the officer; he and I had worked together as Border Patrolmen in Chula Vista, California nine years before! I honestly believe to this day that my position at Morgan, Montana would have been next to impossible to fill, thus the reason for my non-selection at East Port, Idaho. Looking back now, I'm glad that we didn't get the assignment. Things worked out better the way it happened.

It was transfer time. I received notification mid-summer 1970 that we had been selected for Blaine, Washington. We gave any entry on duty date of the middle of October, 1970. Our tour of duty at Morgan, Montana was almost exactly three years, somewhat longer than my predecessors who served around two years. Naturally, one didn't learn much at a small port and in essence was just treading water. I can't say that it was not an enjoyable experience: we made many friends and probably had more company than we do now.

Not only was Al Ganter, representing U.S. Customs, my colleague, co-partner, co-worker but we became great friends and hunted together several seasons for antelope during our off-hours. In fact, Al made a presentation to me in the form of a plaque replete with horns of the last antelope that I had shot with the date and place my last hunting season of 1970. It still hangs in a special place in my den. Al and his wife Louise have long since passed away. I still appreciate how he took me under his wing and apprised me of what I needed to know about U.S. Customs.

Immigration Inspector - Blaine, Washington

Married for a little over eleven years, with two children and 10 moves under our belt we headed for Blaine, Washington. Proceeding up highway I-5, north from Seattle, Washington about 125 miles north we encountered a highway sign, "Blaine next two exits" alluding to a town of some size. At that time, Blaine was probably under 3,000 in population. As we drove into town, we could view the boat marina with scores of both private and commercial fishing vessels and the Georgia Strait. The lights of White Rock, British Columbia were almost dead ahead across the bay, north and a little west about 5 miles.

We found out later that this community was at least twice the size around the turn of the century when logging, lumber and shake mills and fishing comprised the major industries. At that time, Blaine had one of the largest salmon fisheries and canneries in the North West. Lumber from the old-growth trees was shipped to California to held rebuild San Francisco after the earthquake of 1906.

Blaine also had a reputation of which we were unaware but were soon to find out: 'Sin City' was the moniker given to the town. Everyone in this part of northwest Washington and probably all of the residents of British Columbia and the environs had reason for this: Blaine had two adult movie houses and an adult book store, and at one time had several massage parlors. Add this to the eight or ten bars (beer joints) with live music on weekends and a formidable attraction is born. Friday and Saturdays at the border were busy with carloads of fun-seekers who obviously made up a good deal of the statistics at the border. For years, British Colombia had Sunday 'blue laws' which meant that the province was closed to bar drinking on Sundays.

I haven't heard the term 'Sin City" used for years to depict Blaine. After a number of years, probably in the 80's, the Sunday 'blue laws' were stricken from the laws of British Columbia so the residents of the Province imbibed at home on Sundays. The town fathers of Blaine eradicated the massage parlors before they achieved a foothold. As for the adult entertainment- the beer parlors resisted the changing times, and as long as they had pull tabs (paper slot machines) they seemed to get along. Then along came the Native American casinos (at present day there are 4 casinos within 30 miles of Blaine) and with their glitz stole the show from the bars. Live music, bars and everything that went with them gradually died out. Could MADD have had an impact on the drinking in bars with ensuing DUIs? Good chance it did. Nevertheless, Blaine has been a nice, quiet, mostly law abiding community for years now.

My transfer to Blaine, Washington was one of three vacancies that were filled. One of the transferees was an immigration examiner from Los Angeles and the other was an inspector from Guam. Of the contingent of three, I came on first. The other two came several weeks later. Inspections on the line, primary inspection, was shared with our sister agency, U.S. Customs of the Treasury Department. The Agriculture Department had one representative, affectionately call the 'bug man.' He had no primary inspection duties.

We had a contingent of about 20 officers, plus the supervisory inspector in charge and two first line supervisors. U.S. Customs had about twice that number plus two Customs Investigators. The truck customs or commercial port about 1 mile from the main station on I-5, Peace Arch, was mainly manned by Customs. We furnished two men for non-commercial inspections, one on each day shift and evening shift. At the Peace Arch we had three auto traffic lanes and a bus lane.

In no way did we have the technology in the early 70s as that now available; however, that is not to say we were not improvisational. An unknown officer came up with the idea of the EZ PEEK CAR SPOTTER (for which he probably received an incentive award of several hundred dollars). On primary (traffic) inspection we had lookouts written on scraps of paper, and yes, even on our hands. The EZ PEEK CAR SPOTTER was to eliminate this old method of lookout identification. This contraption was made of two pieces of thin hard cardboard about 2 ½" X 4" between which sandwiched dividers numbered from 1 to 9. The idea was to post wanted license plate numbers in each designation according to the first number of the lookout licensed plate. Do you understand this jewel? Most officers didn't and in short time it was history. Back to notes on hands and scraps of paper.

For many years primary inspection conducted on the traffic lanes at Blaine was without benefit of shelter, i.e. no inspection booths! In late 1969 a consensus was reached by U.S. Customs and U.S. Immigration management to approve unheated inspection booths for the officers to utilize while awaiting traffic. All inspections had to been accomplished outside same. In trying to beat the system, a rather eccentric officer of ours put a strain on the system by placing his hat on and stepping out to inspect the auto and its passengers, then he would step back in the booth, take his cap off, as the next car pulled up then he would repeat the process. By the way, sometimes there were a number of vehicles in line to be inspected. I don't recall how this played out with management; it wasn't SOP and he was one of the inspectors who was replaced when he retired.

During the summer months primary inspection at the Peace Arch was mostly pleasant, except for the prevailing south-westerly winds that we often had that wafted the smoke and haze that needed to be endured that blew from the city dump just ½ mile away. Also, since the booths were not heated the wind, rain and cold of winter were difficult.

In 1970 border crossers at both the Peace Arch and Pacific Highway (truck customs) were averaging 2.5 million to 3.0 million. The busiest time of the year was when school was out, from about June 5th to September 1. We had about six school teachers (Immigration) who were called 'seasonals,' working during the months that schools were out for the summer. Customs had a like amount. From September to the end of May, by 9:00 p.m. during the week traffic was down to one lane (and sporadic at that). On weekends, particularly during holidays, multiple traffic lanes were manned later.

We had a number of old-timers in Immigration. They had been there for years, ambition long gone, having found a home with no intent of leaving. But they had acquired the necessary skills required of journeymen inspectors and they did what they were required to do. With this in mind, one could 'shine' at work without any competition. One inspector had a Master's degree in chemical engineering but had been an inspector for at least 25 years. Another had a college degree and had been the police chief in Blaine many years before. He started his Service career in Alaska and eventually retired from here with 30 plus years. Another was a retiree from the Marines with many years work with Immigration. None of our old-timers that I can remember had nicknames. This was not the case of our U.S. Customs co-workers.

To name a few that I remember, there were names like: The Baz, Red, White and Blue, Tok, Doc, The Ghost that Walks, Pruney (remember the Dick Tracy character of that name?), then there was Whispering Phil (with all the doors in the building closed you could hear him conducting his inspections) and Black Bart. I haven't put real names with these characters for a reason. The final two are definitely too unflattering to identify: The Geek and the Chink.

We had only four diagonal parking spaces in front of the building and as the persons referred in for secondary inspection for travel documentation or more in-depth questioning or clients of Customs could be seen as

---

¹The old town dump is now a beautiful park with walking paths, amphitheatre, salmon sculptures & Orca whales half-buried depicting them leaping from the sea. When little our grand kids called it the dead whale park.

While Patrolling Backwards

they passed by the windows. When a person entered the swinging doors Customs was left and Immigration was right. One evening, one of our long-duration officers and known for his eccentricities was waiting for an Oriental-looking gentleman who had just passed by our office window. Our officer greeted this person as he walked with, "Ah so, ah so," (a polite how're you doing?) Needless to say, it wasn't meant to be polite but a way of deriding the prospective entrant. Anyway, the individual answered in no uncertain terms: "Don't call me an asshole!"

This same eccentric inspector, in a room full of people seeking admission to the U.S. mostly of oriental extraction, held up and Korean passport and hollered unnecessarily as loud as he could "Sum Fuk Kim," the name of the individual he would be assisting. This elicited little response except embarrassment by his co-workers.

By the way, the aforementioned officer was dead-set against booze and cigarettes. It just so happened that at our Pacific Highway crossing (truck customs) all the duty free stores were located and purveyed both liquor and cigarettes and tobacco products, which could be purchased without taxes as long as the product was consumed in Canada. Many people took advantage of this situation: Purchased their products at the duty free store, went north a short distance and returned to the United States (we had an expression "flag poling") via the Peace Arch and neglecting to declare the purchases. The officer of whom I am referring was notable in finding the undeclared purchases and at least several times during the shift you would see him heading into customs with a bottle in each hand and non-declaring individual in tow.

In the early 70s young people 'hippies' as it were, were on the move. Naturally, we got our share of both U.S. citizens and Canadian young people on their way south. No problem if you were a citizen of the United States and had proper identification or could sustain that fact. However, all 'hippies' (also called long-hairs) were referred inside for not only Immigration but for Customs inspection, for what I called the 17 dollar wedding The lady who would become Pierre Trudeau's wife was one of the traveling 'hippies' who was a lucky winner of the 17 dollar wedding.

It was not uncommon that a good share of the so-called "hippies" that were referred inside for a more in-depth inspection by U.S. Immigration (were young Canadian citizens with little ID, but claiming they were U.S. citizens.) In just such cases we devised a four or five line paragraph that we

---

[2]Remember Al Capp's Lil' Abner? The 17 dollar wedding meant the works. In U.S. Customs lingo meant sans clothing, 'skin search.'

had the individual read. Interspersed in the paragraph were words that had different English (our) pronunciation, such as sofa - chesterfield; napkins - servietes; lieutenant - leftenant; and the letter Z, which Canadians pronounce as 'zed'. A true Canadian was hard-pressed to use the American English word. To cap off the paragraph: "Now I have passed my test from A to Z". Sometimes they used the American pronunciations correctly all the way through, but would slip up and say, "Now I have passed my test from A to Zed". After flubbing up the paragraph they were generally directed back to Canada.

In those long-ago days of the 70s there was a "hippie" weekly alternative newspaper called the Georgia Straight, printed in Vancouver, Canada. The bottom third of the front page of the paper was a column entitled, "Busted Heads." listing all the "hippies" who had been proudly arrested/convicted in the Vancouver mainland area for possession of marijuana. It just so happened that the Walter- McCarran Immigration Act of 1952 precluded the admission of illegal aliens who had been convicted of such crimes. Needless to say, this gave us a rich pool of excludable "hippies" whom we daily refused admission to.

It seemed that in the 'hippie' generation that there was a lack of respect for all law enforcement, which included us inspectors at the border. On a daily basis we were called f...... pigs by these young people on the go. One night, unbeknownst to U.S. Immigration supervisors, we made a huge banner out of butcher paper and printed thereon P I G S. Under P we printed 'ride'; under I we printed 'integrity' and between G and S we printed 'uts' Spelled out then, was Pride, Integrity and Guts. We disposed of the sign before we left shift that night.

On April 21, 1972 our second daughter, Andrea Lee was born at St. Joseph's Hospital, in Bellingham, Washington. Another momentous occasion for the Hattery family!

I made a friend for life one evening as I relieved the 4:00pm to 12 midnight officer at the Peace Arch. As I approached the building a pink Cadillac almost tailgated by a black and white Mountie police car. Both vehicles headed into Blaine. The office I relieved informed me he had admitted the Mountie as a visitor for business; I can't remember for sure what status he had admitted the Cadillac driver. I quickly ascertained that what had transpired was not copasetic and I quickly contacted Border Patrol by radio, gave him a run-down, and asked him to have both vehicles

---

[3] In one point in history Pierre Trudeau was the Prime Minister of Canada.

[4] One of the Beatles was held for exclusion in NY in early 70s, under this statute but a lawyer got him off because in England, one could be convicted without certain ramifications.

returned to the Port. Shortly thereafter, both vehicles arrived at the Port and the drivers alit from their cars. The occupants were, one a young Mountie in his early 20s and the driver of the Cadillac, a large male of apparently good shape, in his 40s. When I asked the young Mountie why he chased a car into the United States he told me that the miscreant had been speeding southbound on the freeway near White Rock, Canada. I explained to the young man that he could cause an international incident by doing what he did and I questioned him about his authority and as to what was he going to put on the ticket for place of arrest. Standing there and taking it all in was the Cadillac driver. The Mountie called him over out of my earshot and I suppose read him the riot act, got in his patrol car and made a left around the building headed for Canada.

The speeder turned out to be one of several Canadians who were professional wrestlers who lived in Blaine and were permanent residents of the United States. Thanking me profusely he said that he had just come back from Vancouver, where he had wrestled, headed home on the freeway absent-mindedly going faster than the speed limit. He said that he saw the red lights of the Mountie car but didn't stop figuring he could safely make it to the border. Ever since the above incident, lead-footed Gene Kiniski, driver of the pink Cadillac, would always wave or greet me on the street.

I've never been a great one for remembering names, but one of U.S. Customs long-time inspectors, notorious for his WWII stories after having been a Pearl Harbor survivor and a life-long resident of Blaine, introduced me to his new Customs Port Director, a Mr. Wataname, Japanese-American. The very next day when we were heading for the parking lot, Mr. Watanabe was headed for work as well as one of our U.S. Immigration supervisors, who had yet to meet the new U.S. Customs Port Director. The aforementioned U.S. Customs officer, minding his manners, introduced his new boss, Mr. Wataname to my supervisor, as Mr. Yamamoto. Immediately I knew a faux pas when I saw one, but didn't correct the U.S. Customs officer. Out of ear-shot of his new boss as we walked away, he said "Do you know what I did? I introduced Mr. Wataname as Mr. Yamamoto. He's the one who led the attack on Pearl Harbor." Not a word was said of this gaffe, and Mr. Wataname obviously took it good naturedly, and turned out to be liked by everyone.

It doesn't take much to get a joke started and I was the butt of this one.

---

[5]In the 1950s Gene Kiniski was an outstanding college football player and became a professional wrestler, referee and manager. He wrestled before steroids hit the street. He maintained fitness in retirement. He passed away several years ago. He was a great friend to everyone.

One evening, two gentlemen approached the counter after being referred inside. One was Jamaican carrying that country's passport with a non-immigrant visitor's visa issued by our Consulate. His companion was from Czechoslovakia carrying that country's passport but did not have a visitor's visa. They were just going into Blaine to enjoy the town. I politely told the Jamaican that he appeared to be admissible, but his friend the Czechoslovakian needed a visa. There was some whining and begging going on and relentless to a degree. Several times that night these two came into the office and tried and tried for me to change my mind with no luck. At change of shift at midnight as we were walking out the door a Border Patrolman drove around the north end of the building and he asked "how was everything going?" About that time, the two with whom I had the repeated confrontations appeared and began the pleading again for the third or fourth time, when one my colleagues told the Border Patrolman that I had been aggravated by these guys all night. The guy lacking the visa proffered his passport to the Border Patrolman and gave him the same whiney plea as he had given me. The Patrolman opened the back door of his sedan (quite forcefully) and commanded them to either return to Canada or get in his patrol car. This was not done to the satisfaction of the officer who then used force to get their attention and they turned left around the building in their auto and left for Canada. I never saw them again. However, to my chagrin, the joke, "Did you hear about Hattery getting his Czech cancelled?" made the rounds.

My efforts have been to recount or elucidate somewhat immigration history at the various places that I have had the opportunity to work. But there were two instances at the Blaine Port of Entry of a commendable nature accomplished by officers of our sister agency, U.S. Customs that need to be recounted.

In the early summer of 1973 as I recall, an individual approached the inspection lanes of the port, and as he stopped, the U.S. citizen made a negative declaration to the Customs officer. To verify or check the veracity of the declaring individual, traveling alone, nothing visible in the auto or trunk out of order except a pair of old beat-up large stereo speakers. The driver was unable to state conclusively, when, where, and how they came into his possession. The Customs officer handed the individual a referral slip and told him to take same inside to customs secondary to make peace with the officer awaiting inside.

Plopping the speakers on the counter and handing the referral slip to the Customs officer awaited the officer's reply. Noting that the screws on the back of the speakers had recently been fooled with, the officer reached into the tool drawer, pulled out a screw driver, asking the owner of the speakers to unscrew the backs of each of the speakers. This evoked a decidedly visible nervous condition in the individual, with sweat beads popping out on his forehead. Having a terrible time in this condition to place the screw driver properly, finally did after some finagling. If one will excuse the old expression, "He was as nervous as a whore in church." Exposed to the light of day and the Customs officer, celluloid packets of heroin filled the inner recesses of both the speakers. Customs Agents arrived on the scene, arrested and hand-cuffed the individual and took with them what amounted what amounted to over 1/2 million dollars in drugs.

Just a few months later, in hot summer, and the involvement of the above secondary Customs officer - this time on primary traffic this time had a young lady in her early 30's drive up in his lane. The car, a junky nondescript old clunker, usually driven by persons of slight means, sat the driver matching the condition of the automobile. There was detritus in both the front and back seat of the automobile throw carelessly about. The trunk was in much the same condition and disarray. What stuck out like a sore thumb were what appeared to be one-gallon dark colored Clorox bottles filled with liquid laying helter-skelter in the back of the car and in the trunk, possibly near a dozen in all. The owner of the vehicle disclaimed ownership of and would not disclose anything about the booty. The astute officer opened one bottle, and the contents, a viscous substance spewed out on the pavement. It developed after Customs Agents came on the scene that the liquid in the gallon jars or jugs was liquid hash, to the tune of nearly one million dollars in street value. The Customs Inspectors in both cases were appropriately commended. Their employment with U.S. Customs was doubly assured. Both of them are retired from U.S. Customs with many years of commendable service.

Work as an inspections officer at Blaine was seldom hum-drum. People and new instances were part of the job and one never knew what the day would bring.

What a surprise I got when my boss at the Peace Arch called me one morning in mid December, 1969, while my wife and I were having coffee, informing me that I had been selected for promotion to criminal investigator in the district office at Omaha, Nebraska. We would be leaving Blaine in 30 days or so, not ever thinking we would return.

Criminal Investigator - Omaha, Nebraska

Reporting-in day was about the 15th of January, 1974. It was probably around 15 degrees, but far from the cold temperatures of northeastern Montana. I had already called the District Director and thanked him for selecting me for the investigator slot before we left Blaine. I immediately took a liking to my new boss and thanked him again in person. My new boss was a laid-back, avuncular individual with a rich background in Immigration; he was immediately friendly and greeted me with a hearty handshake. I could sense that he was concerned about my family and in particular about our finding a home. Before I left his office he told me to not worry about work until the family was settled. What a great way to start a new job.

We were to find out about the extremes in temperature: cold, snowy winters and hot summers. Spring and fall were nice but they were also the seasons for tornados. I would to learn more about the impact of weather on my life later.

The District Director had me shadow a more experienced investigator, who showed me the ropes and who became one of my best friends. It was six months or so before I felt comfortable in doing investigations solo. At the time of my entry on duty in Omaha we had four investigators, one of whom was a trainee. We had all the entire states of Nebraska and Iowa as our responsibility. Freeway I-80 wended its way through most of Nebraska and all of Iowa. The distance we were assigned to cover was over 425 miles from Omaha to Scottsbluff, Nebraska and the territory from Omaha to the Mississippi River on the east was about 325 miles. From just referrals from the State Police in both those states we were kept busy following up on the many referrals from them, generally in the form of undocumented Mexican citizens who had been smuggled into this country by professional smugglers. The smugglers charged them as much as $5000 per head which included transportation to points east via I-80. Usually they were smuggled across the U.S/Mexico border in California and Arizona and brought to safe houses on the U.S. side for subsequent transportation north.

Usually the troopers from Nebraska and Iowa would stop a late model pickup with a camper or motor home for some traffic violation to use for probable cause in the search for dope smuggling, at which time they would encounter fifteen to twenty non-English speaking individuals. We would be

---

[7] I found out later (not from him) that he was a WWII Navy veteran and had won the Silver Star for gallantry beyond the call of duty as a Navy pilot.

contacted via our answering service after hours that would begin our questioning of all these non-English speaking individuals as the trooper put them on the phone, one by one so we could "wet" them down before we could authorize their being held for us. This telephone quiz in Spanish could take up to three hours, sometimes in the middle of the night. These poor old campesinos with little education or knowledge of telephones would sometimes need assistance from the trooper even on the use of the phone. Every once in a while you would hear them being berated, "Dammit! Turn the phone around!"

One particular smuggling case that stands out in my mind was referred to us by trooper Messerschmidt out of North Platte, Nebraska on I-80. It was a hot July day in 1976. The trooper spotted a late-model pickup with a large camper installed tooling east down I-80 with a slight rear end drag. I don't recall the probable cause that prompted the trooper to stop the vehicle, but probably the back-end tilt had something to do with it. The trooper was astonished when he had the driver open the rear door. The front of the truck (double cab) held at least eight adults and the camper contained about six or eight females and possibly six to eight young children, from infants to ages four or five. We were told that the stench was so bad that he

---

[7] "wet" is short for wetback (slang). Meaning to determine their illegality. Wetback is a racial slur referring to Mexicans. The term originates from Operation Wetback. In 1949 the Border Patrol seized nearly 280,000 illegal immigrants. By 1953, the numbers had grown to more than 865,000, and the U.S. government felt pressured to do something about the onslaught of immigration. What resulted was Operation WetBack.

almost threw up. All of these people were crammed into this vehicle. The only facilities that they had for toileting needs were gallon milk jugs. The temperature inside the camper was nearly 100 degrees! We were almost 275 miles east of North Platte, Nebraska when alerted, but we hastily sped to the jail where they all were being held over three hours later.

After arrival in North Platte, we quickly separated the men from the women. The men stayed in jail and the women and children, possibly 20 in all, were put up in an old turn-of-the-century hotel, where we brought them groceries and disposable diapers. The sheriff was Luis Trujillo and his wife, whose name I don't recall, were like angels. The sheriff's wife got on the local radio and made a plea for these unfortunates for donations of clothing of all sorts. The outpouring of charity was unbelievable.

It took us some time to process this man's inhumanity to man. The smugglers had charged them several thousands of dollars each to be smuggled across the border near Tijuana, Mexico and to transport them to wherever they could find work, upwards of two thousand miles in the direction of Chicago. They had been promised that if they didn't
give any information to Immigration in the event they were detected, they would be given the next trip free. What a scam! We were several days in North Platte.

I don't recall getting a prosecution on this case. We, however, did secure bus passage on the Trailways bus (for the women and children) that just happened to have a stop at the hotel. So one bright early sun-shiny day the bus pulled up and the driver, with a smile on his face, greeted us with "Good morning." He hadn't heard the pandemonium of all the kids and their mothers yet, and he didn't know yet of the avalanche of boxes and paraphernalia they had acquired from all the good Samaritans. Anyway, we told the driver we had a few passengers for him. His smile turned to a grimace when he opened the door to the hotel and saw what confronted him...yelling kids and a mountain of boxes. This particular case was presented to the U.S. Attorney for prosecution, but if I recall correctly prosecution was denied. The Mexican men in this group were processed sepa-

---

[8] The reason I recall the sheriff's name was because of the great kindness he and his wife exhibited towards these unfortunate Mexican people. Also, with great sadness I recall that the Sheriff's son was night manager of the Holiday Day Inn in Des Moines, Iowa was murdered by a person on work release from prison shortly after this smuggling operation.

[9] In my experience with the U.S. Attorney in cases such as this: non-English speaking Hispanics and numerous witnesses were anathema. The prosecutors cringed at the thought of conducting a trial through an interpreter and securing witnesses for an indeterminate amount of time.

rately and voluntarily returned to Mexico apart from their families.

One day we received a call from a rather distraught female complaining that her Mexican boyfriend in his twenties was just laying around and not seeking employment and she was fed up with this arrangement. She had called from her place of employment. She told me that he was in their apartment in downtown Omaha right then, doing what he normally did - nothing. Taking time on this complaint, just a few short blocks from our office, would take little time, so my partner and I went to the address she had given me, a two story walkup apartment. Knocking on the door got no response. As we were walking away from the door, just below us at the front stoop, here came our suspect, matching the description she had given. He saw us almost immediately, threw a sack of groceries over his shoulder and fled the scene. By the time we got to the sidewalk in front of the apartment he had disappeared. We surmised that he had fled west on the street and made a left turn into a large parking area that contained a drug store chain and a super market. Nowhere to be seen, we knew he must have run into either the drugstore or the supermarket. No luck in the drugstore. I started towards the rear of the store and worked forward while my partner began in the front. All of a sudden I heard, "Someone jumped over the turnstile!" My partner and I ended a hot foot race by overpowering the individual several blocks away. His next stop was our office for paper work, thence his voluntary return to Mexico. The reason I remember about this individual is that about one month later he was back in Omaha, apparently leading the same lazy life as he had been before. He was probably with the same women who had previously reported him, when at a rowdy dance in south Omaha one Saturday night he got in a knife/gun fight over some female, when he came out second best. He was shot in the abdomen and hospitalized for some time, paralyzed from the waist down for life. The Immigration Service was not responsible for his hospital bill, but did eventually pay for a nurse when he was air-lifted by private aircraft back to Mexico. I still think about this guy's life of despair in his home country.

My partner and I worked together at different times and when we had a project together either I would pick him up as he only lived a few blocks away or he would do the same for me. This particular morning he picked me up and announced that he was going to shave his head, or what remained of his hair. Not wanting to dissuade him I told him, "Hey, you'll look great, do it." He was late picking me up one morning, and apparently shaved his head in a hurry. He had pieces of toilet paper stuck around and on his head apparently to staunch the blood where he had nicked himself while shaving. Every morning when we arrived at the office there was a sucker awaiting him at his desk, in apparent reference to his Kojack-like appearance. No one 'fessed up to this deed!

On April 25, 1975 the war in Vietnam was over and we capitulated in Saigon. Just prior to that date, on April 3, 1975, President Gerald R. Ford announced "Operation Baby Lift ", which would evacuate about 2,000 orphans from that country. In addition to the 2,000 orphans evacuated by Baby Lift, operation New Life resulted in the evacuation of over of over 110,000 Vietnamese refugees. Then our work began.

Our job as investigators was to photograph, fingerprint and identify all the potential adoptive parents and their wards. We were also detailed as examiners to interview all the refugees that had taken up residence in Nebraska or Iowa. It was most heartwarming to meet and greet the prospective parents of these orphans. Two particular cases are still particularly vivid in my memory: A Nebraska State senator made the most of an adoption he and his wife were in the process of accomplishing by interviews in all the media. What a splash it made in the news. It just so happened that the sitting state senator was in the midst of a political campaign for his re-election. Their prospective adoptee was a girl of about 10 years of age. If my recollection is correct, he lost the election. After having this young Vietnamese girl in their home for nearly a year, they apparently didn't need the publicity of good Samaritans any longer for his political career so they sent her back to the adoption agency.

The other case that I remember included a rather young couple in Iowa who had two very young girls. The husband dearly wanted a boy, so they proceeded to adopt a Vietnamese boy three or four years old. I was quite impressed with this couple, their marriage and the successful farm operation that they shared. I made more than one call on them over three or four months and I was quite happy for them. The greatest share of the Vietnamese Baby Lift were actually orphans. However, it just so happened, that the mother of the young boy this couple eventually adopted showed up. She had flown out from Saigon on a separate airplane and eventually found her young son. To be an orphan a child one has to have lost both parents, or if one survives that surviving parent has to irrevocably give the child up for adoption. This mother did not in any way give her son up for adoption, and of course the courts considered this and annulled the adoption to the Iowa couple.

1975 was a banner year for storms . Almost to the day, one year from the date of my entry on duty in Omaha we had a blizzard to end all blizzards

---

[10]One of the C-5A Galaxys involved in the operation planes crashed, killing 138 passengers.

While Patrolling Backwards

on January 10 - 11. It had been snowing all day. We were finally released from work about noon or so on the 10th of January, a Friday as the blizzard built up steam. We were the last of the government agencies to be excused because of the weather. The Army Corps of Engineers were the first.

In order to get home, we used the government van and headed westward on I-80 out to western Omaha to first drop off a co-worker. Two of my colleagues were with me and our secretary. One colleague drove in blinding snowy wind-blown conditions. The wipers on the vehicle were useless. In an attempt to keep the windshield clear in front of him, he futilely used a scraper. As the visibility became less and less, we were concerned obviously, of our safety. After losing the scraper out of his hand, the driver had to stick his head out the side window to see somewhat. In doing so, his hair was blown back and frozen in that position. Funny now. Not funny then. He looked like the Mad Russian. We got to one of the investigators' homes and dropped him off. I don't know why we didn't stay. We headed north from there, but eventually, say within five miles, we were stuck on the side of the road, unable to go further. We hitched a ride from a Samaritan to a service station on Dodge Street, still miles from our homes. The station was packed with humanity. Fortunately, within walking distance from the station we found warmth and security where we spent the night at a home of one our co-workers. The storm subsided the next day but what a moonscape prevailed! There must have been at least four feet of snow everywhere one looked. The Army National Guard had to use their 6-wheel drive vehicles for rescue of stranded persons. It was late afternoon when I got home a full day from when were excused from work. The snow in my driveway drifted to over six feet.

Just four months later, May 6, 1975, at a 3:33 p.m. to 3:50 p.m. a devastating tornado hit Omaha. It touched down in northern Sarpy County just south of Omaha and it moved north, northeast through residential and business areas of west central Omaha lifting over the northern section of the city. There was extensive damage to apartments, homes, schools, autos, trucks and trees. In some locations the damage area was ¼ mile wide. Damage estimates ranged from $250 million to $500 million. The number of houses destroyed was 287 with damage to 1400 others. Three people did perish. An elderly women died in her home and likely did not hear the warnings. A waitress was killed as she huddled with others in a restroom. A man was killed while seeking shelter at a service station. If the tornado

---

[11]See 1975 January & May 6 complete stories in Omaha World Herald.

57

had touched down 30 minutes before, innumerable children would have been killed or injured at the elementary school they attended. This school and the apartment complex home of our naturalization examiner were the first places that were touch-down sites by the storm.

Our son's school sustained substantial roof damage. On his birthday, school was out until September. He had already departed from school and was at home huddled under our over-turned couch in our basement with our youngest daughter at the storms apex. The storm missed our neighborhood by about 10 blocks. My wife and older daughter were at a Campfire meeting in the vicinity scared out of their wits! Our three-year-old daughter was so traumatized by this event that it was several years before she was no longer frightened by sirens of emergency vehicles.

Our naturalization examiner was the only unlucky one in our office to suffer loss due to this disaster. After several days, he was allowed into his apartment to check on his things. Lo and behold, the tornado was rather discriminating in damage to his personal effects with the exception that the suction of the tornado vacuumed his clothes from his closet and crammed them under the mattress of his bed. For several days after this episode, he would excitedly explain to anyone who would listen, the details of this voodoo wind. One day, one of the so-called rapt listeners said to him, "Come on Terry, tell us the truth - that's how you press your clothes." He of course re-explained everything, ad infinitum.

During Easter week of 1975, myself and our young trainee were detailed to the quad-cities area: Betandorf, Davenport, Moline and East Moline, Illinois to check on the status of foreign students who were attending the 3-year course at the Palmer School of Chiropractic. A good third of the student population at the school were matriculated from Canada, South Africa, New Zealand and Australia. Information that we had on hand, was that most of the foreign students were employed full-time (without Service permission) on the evening shift at various occupations and going to school from 7:00 a.m. to 3 p.m.

Before departing for eastern Iowa we perused foreign student files in the files room and made a list of all those who had applied for employment authorization and were denied. Keep in mind, work authorization was not automatic. In fact, before a foreign student is admitted, he/she must establish to the inspecting officer that they have or have access to funds for at least one year without having to work. If it can be established after one year that circumstances beyond their control are present, permission can be

---

[12]The storm hit on my son's 15th birthday, tearing the roof off of the school he attended. The school year ended until it resumed in September.

given for no more than 20 hours per week when school is in session. Permission for full-time employment can be given during summer break.

As it turned out, I think that we rubbed these prospective aspiring chiropractors the wrong way. We determined that nearly 50 students violated the terms of their admission by working. And we wrote them up as SEBAF - a code word meaning working without Service permission, fingerprinted them and awaited from our Regional Office permission to issue them each with an order to show cause as to why they should not be deported. By Regional policy, we sent all the paperwork including their passports for higher-up approval. The Regional Commissioner sat on all this stuff, giving a majority of these violators slack enough for them to finish their studies and return to their home countries, with their passports in hand. None of these students met a judge for a deportation hearing. At least, I think we did a commendable job in protecting domestic employment.

Another hot summer afternoon in July or August of 1976 I received a call from the Iowa State Police regarding a vehicle that a trooper had stopped just east of Des Moines, Iowa on Interstate 80. This was about 145 miles from Omaha. It took me nearly 2 ½ hours to arrive where the aliens had been taken to this small jail facility run by the Sheriff.

I could hardly believe my eyes when I saw what I had to deal with. It seems that these Mexican males, about fifteen of them in all, had had a third party buy them a communal vehicle in Juarez, Mexico; he drove it across for them where they picked it up on the U.S. side and had traveled nonstop except for gas and food, to the point where they had been stopped some 1500 miles distant from the border.

How this old dilapidated run-down large model Buick or Oldsmobile held so many people and got so far I will never know! The back seat had been discarded which opened up the back clear through to the trunk. At least four of them sat in the front seat and the others either lay or sat down in the back seat area and into the trunk. It took me hours to process each of them. While in detention the sheriff's wife coddled these guys like they were her children. I am sure they had never been treated so well or had such meals served to them as they did.

This particular incident was just the tip of the iceberg. The other investigators had their fair share of similar referrals. In my wildest dreams before coming to Omaha I never thought that the Omaha district, Nebraska and Iowa, would be so inundated with illegal Mexicans; every packing house and poultry processing plant had more than their share. The I-80 freeway held a continuous stream of illegal Mexicans following whatever course that they could get employment. They were met by employers who readily hired them with open arms. To this day, it seems like Congress couldn't care less about the more than 10 million illegal aliens now residing in our country.

I was on call for the week in early summer of 1976 when I received a call from our answering service on a Saturday afternoon regarding twenty Mexican males who were in custody in the Lincoln County jail in Lincoln, Nebraska. A confirmation call to the jail revealed the prior information, but also that these twenty bodies needed to be taken into custody and out of their facility, as there was standing room only. Unable to contact either of the detention guards, I picked up the government van and proceeded to haul these individuals in several trips to the Sarpy County jail in Papillion, Nebraska where they always had plenty of room. The one-way trip to Lincoln, Nebraska from Omaha, Nebraska was a little over 40 miles. To shorten the story somewhat, it took me from Saturday afternoon until after 4:00 p.m. on Sunday before I had completed all the paperwork.

Another time I received a call from a jailer from a turn-of-the-century jail in Sidney, Nebraska announcing that he too was cramped for space and the seventeen Mexican males had to be picked up and placed in a facility more accommodating. I can't recall how these individuals got in his jail, but unequivocally they had to be moved. The nearest facility that we used was at Scottsbluff, Nebraska, 90 miles distant. Then again,
I was over 425 miles away in Omaha. After traveling over 8 hours by government vehicle from Omaha, I was able to transport these aliens in several trips from Sidney, Nebraska to Scottsbluff, Nebraska. I drove at breakneck speed to get the job done. If I had been clocked it would have shown my speed well above the limit posted.

Shortly after I received a call from a detective in North Platte, Nebraska concerning a shotgun shooting of a Mexican alien, I was on my way bag and baggage to interview the fourteen Mexicans they had incarcerated as material witnesses at a shooting in front of an apartment building over the week-end. It was quite time-consuming, interviewing all these purported material witnesses. Right off the bat it was determined that all the Mexicans they had in custody were employed in the local meat packing plant. A cursory interview revealed that they all had entered the United States illegally, which meant a tremendous amount of paper work for deportation preparation. They all lived in a run-down, ratty apartment building in a neighborhood to match.

Most of the aliens whom I interviewed were not eye witnesses to the

---

[13]Scottsbluff, Nebraska was part of the Oregon Trail that pioneers trekking west winched their wagons down the precipitous escarpment. Chimney rock near Scottsbluff was a natural phenomenon that pioneers zeroed in on.

shooting, but obviously privy to what had happened. Dances were regular weekend events in communities such as North Platte, frequented usually by hot-blooded young Mexican males, where beer drinking, carousing, fighting over the women was standard fare. As it happened, drinking, carousing and fighting over a woman was the cause of this jealous fight. As it was related to me, a more macho man took the love of the other's women - taking her home, as it were. The jilted person went looking for his nemesis, and obviously knew where he lived. Having a friend take him in his car and arming himself with a shotgun, went to this rabbit-warren, scabby apartment and called out for the taker of his love from the passenger side of the car, at the curb at the sidewalk. Several Mexican males came out to see what was going on, and right behind them was the person he was seeking. In a blink of an eye a shotgun blast roared from the car blasting the individual in the face, killing him instantly. It was a dark night, no street light and witnesses could not readily identify the shooter. Obviously the automobile took off post- haste!

After a lengthy process and a lot of circumstantial evidence, the shooter was brought before a judge at a preliminary (probable cause) hearing the next day. Guess who did the interpreting. There must have been at least 25 or 30 Mexican people (I assumed were permanent residents) from the community sitting in on this process. Neither of the attorneys, defense nor prosecution, took into account the fact that I was not a native Spanish speaker, but did their questioning in I what I thought was a rather rapid manner. It seemed as though none of their questions were simple yes or no, but rather lengthy. Fortunately, I got through the process of interpreting without a peep from the audience.

Just shortly after returning back to Omaha, the detective with whom I worked called me with some news…it seems that the shooter got to thinking about the grim circumstances if he were convicted. A day or so after the hearing, the court-appointed attorney brought his client before the judge on a hearing on bond reduction. His client blurted out, without counsel from his attorney, that he was guilty and he had killed the other man out of jealousy. Immediately, the judge scolded the defendant telling him that this was not the time or place for such a plea, and that he should confer with his attorney before making such a plea. The long and short of it was that the defendant was accorded a proper venue at another time and place for his plea. He eventually received a 25-year sentence. I was jubilant that my services would no longer be needed for trial.

My speediness in that particular incident reminds me of the time we were all in the office on a Monday morning recounting our last week's experiences. My partner, whom I previously mentioned a short time ago, shared with us an incident he was involved in on Interstate 80 in western Nebraska. He told us, "I got stopped for speeding" and I queried, how fast were you going? He said, "About 100." I then asked him, didn't you tell him who you were? "Yes, he said, and that's the reason he didn't throw me in jail." "He made me promise to send him a check in the amount of $60.00 for bail when I got back to Omaha." I felt they didn't need to know about my lead foot.

Along with so-called smuggling cases and other referrals of illegal aliens from police agencies all over Nebraska and Iowa, probably marriage fraud investigations came in a close second. Every spouse petition was referred to investigations to determine marriage the bona fides; usually what we encountered were Mexican males hitched up with gullible females. And oddly enough, most of these type of investigations were centered in Iowa, particularly in Sioux City, Iowa. In my experience I found mostly gullible females who were made to believe that 'Jose' was in love with them. In truth, he was not, and many were living common-law in Mexico with a family or married with a family, obviously unbeknownst to his American bride. Except for the necessities of life, most of the individuals sent their earnings home to Mexico. Third party initiation of these cases for money rarely occurred in this neck of the woods.

"Bed check" was one of our schemes in which we called upon the individuals where they were supposedly living together. Knocking on the door of this kind of rundown apartment with a matching neighborhood I was greeted by a Mexican male with no comprehension of the English language. Questioning him in Spanish and looking the living quarters over through the front door, I asked for permission to come in, and continued my questioning as to his right to be in the U.S. His vague answers to where his spouse was as well as the living area giving no clue to a woman's presence, I handcuffed him and proceeded with him to the local jail.

After sleuthing around, I was able to locate his alleged wife living with her parents in another part of Sioux City. As it turned out, the "blushing bride" was mentally challenged and had been hoodwinked by her alleged husband. I have no doubts that she thought "Jose" loved her. As far as I

---

[14]Public Law 99-639 (Act of 11/10/1986), which was passed to deter immigration-related marriage fraud. Its major provision stipulates that aliens deriving their immigrant status based on a marriage of less than two years are conditional immigrants. To remove their conditional status the immigrants must apply at a U.S. Citizenship and Immigration office during the 90-day period before their second anniversary of receiving conditional status. If the aliens cannot show that the marriage through wich the status was and is a valid one, their conditional immigration status may be terminated and they may become deportable.

could determine, no money was exchanged for this purported marriage. I convinced the "bride" and her parents that it was a serious criminal offense to be connected to such a scam, and that upon conviction of such could mean jail time. It took little encouragement for her to withdraw the petition she had filed for "Jose." It wasn't long before the alien was on his way back to Mexico courtesy of Uncle Sam.

I had a young investigator with me in Sioux City one evening when we made a cold call bed check at an upstairs apartment. A rather large-sized bleached blonde answered the door. Just over her shoulder in the living room was a somewhat portly Mexican-looking male working out with exercise equipment, wearing only jeans, no shirt or shoes. In the wink of an eye, the guy fled thru the kitchen and out the back door-apparently not her husband for whom she had filed a petition. Before I could say anything, the young investigator with a flare in his nostrils and Border Patrol training in his background fled after this guy and through the house. The bleach blonde blew her stack! She was screaming "Where's your search warrant?" lacing her screams with profanity. She slowly discontinued her venting when I told her that if she continued with the search warrant bit, I was going to have to charge her with harboring an illegal alien.

Shortly after, here came my tyro investigator with a big smile on his face with the handcuffed alien in tow. It was just a short chase down the back stairs and to an icy side walk. But, as I found out, the Mexican alien slid on the icy sidewalk catching himself as he fell, breaking his wrist. My partner handcuffed the Mexican over his broken wrist without knowledge that it was broken and by the time they got back to the apartment this guy's wrist was swollen so large that it had covered the cuff. The alien related the whole incident in Spanish about how he fell on the icy sidewalk after being chased. I was hoping that he had been injured at work. No such luck.

This incident curtailed our investigative activities for the evening but entailed our bringing this guy to the emergency ward at the hospital where he was operated on and where he remained for several days. We waited for several hours until this guy was safely in bed. Incidentally, the District Director gave this alien voluntary departure to Mexico. In the ensuing days we arrested several of his friends who came to visit him at the hospital different times.

On not rare occasions, I would receive telephone calls from women who would ask if I remembered when she and her purported husband had visited my office; and did I remember visiting them in Sioux City. She would lament the fact that "Jose" had gone back to Mexico to pick up his immigration visa but she had not seen hide nor hair of him for over a year. I was always blunt with these calls: I would tell them they were duped! Duh.

In Waterloo, Iowa, I made a call to a residence in regard to an individual who had petitioned for his wife from Poland. He lived with his mother, both of Polish extraction and he was a tailor by trade. They lived in a comfortable home, well-furnished and he was apparently successful in his trade. I found out that he no longer wanted to sponsor his wife for permanent residence. His wife apparently gave him an ultimatum: either his mother, with whom he had lived with all his life, would have to go, or she was going. Case closed! He chose his mother. He withdrew his sponsorship of his wife. He assured me that he would pay her way back to Poland - no expense to the government. When I had completed all the paperwork and presented his wife with documentation for her departure he walked me to my car and assured me that on my next trip to Waterloo he would tailor for me a sport coat. I thanked him for this gesture and said thanks but no thanks. I was just doing my job.

One arrest that I was particularly proud of concerned an illegal Mexican alien who had escaped handcuffed custody, apparently assaulting the arresting investigator in the melee who had been my predecessor in Omaha. My informant furnished that she had overheard this individual in a beer-joint in north Sioux City, South Dakota one Saturday night bragging about the events of his escape, of how he assaulted the investigator and fled on foot to south Omaha where he had his handcuffs sawed off, several years ago. Her information revealed his employment at a meat-packing plant in Spenser, Iowa from whence we obtained his vehicle and license number. I placed an all-points bulletin for that individual for central Iowa. Lo and behold I got an after-hours telephone call from an arresting officer early the next morning, which ended in my taking the escapee to a Magistrate near his place of arrest. He ultimately received a short sentence and was subsequently held for Immigration deportation. His reentry after deportation would have been a felony offense.

My colleague, who had about one year altogether behind him as a trainee investigator, was the focus of attention at security at the airport in Omaha, Nebraska in the Spring of 1976. He was accompanying me to meet an airplane on which an individual who was the center of our interest was to arrive and we were to note his arrival without his knowledge of us. Arriving at the airport, we locked our weapons in the glove box of our government car and then made our way to the arrivals gate to peruse the arrival of our quarry. The only obstacle between us and the arrivals area was security. I proceeded first, and went through the X-ray machine placing everything in my pockets on the moving belt with no bells, whistles or horns. Not so for my partner. When the alarm went off I heard the examiner tell him to place everything in his pockets on the moving belt and step through x-ray again. This time, he put several bullets on the belt and tried the process again. No luck! Again he failed the check. By this time our plane blocked and passengers were disembarking. Again he was told to place the contents of his pockets on the belt - again he put several bullets out of his pockets on the belt and failed again! I had no alternative but to leave him at this point and to rush to the gate where I was able to confirm the arrival of our individual. Hurrying back to assist my colleague, I could see what I found out later was the airport manager, several guards and security people surrounding my friend. I got in on the act when one of the security people excitedly exclaimed, "He was with him," pointing to me. When I approached this group I had my identification out, explained to them that we were investigators with the Immigration Service (and apparently my partner had his ID) on a stake-out. This seemed to appease them and they dispersed. I am sure they were wondering why my partner carried a pocketful of .38 caliber ammo, but just didn't bother to ask. As it turned out, when he went home at night he would unload his weapon and pile the bullets on his dresser. The next day he would absent-mindedly forget to reload and obtained new bullets at the office. He had this pocketful of ammo that he had hoarded before returning it to the range officer. To this day, I don't know why he didn't unload everything from his pockets and ID himself properly to begin with. I cringe to think of what would happen at airport security in this day and age.

What happened to all the Gypsies? Surely, my colleague, would have liked to know conclusively. He related to the rest of us investigators in the office one day after receiving a call the evening before during his on-call duties. He and a fellow worker drove out to the rest area on Interstate 80 west of Omaha a few miles. The Nebraska state trooper who called related that he had stopped a caravan of vehicles, autos, pickup campers, motor homes, et cetera, numbering a good dozen or so, all traveling together. Due to some traffic infraction they had been stopped, after which some of the drivers were cited. The individuals appeared to be of the same descent or origin, and all of "gypsy-like" character. He wasn't sure, but thought we would be interested in their group - thus the call. Arriving on the scene, a determination was made that the whole group were ethnic "Gypsies." Due to the passage of time (over 30 years) I am at a loss as to the how, when or where this huge group of illegal aliens entered the United States. Probably they entered in smaller groups through small border ports on the northern border and then joined forces later down the road. What I don't have any doubts about is that my colleague did find that through some subterfuge they had illegally entered the country. And all were of ethic Romanian Gypsy background with no documentation to show their legal status in the

United States.

The trooper called in the early evening on this group and the two investigators dug into collecting data on the spot and preparing the documentation on their illegal status which took hours to accomplish. This amenable, friendly group of shysters - as Gypsies have always been tagged- gladly furnished whatever information they thought was needed. It was late in the evening, so the leader of their group agreed that it had been a long day so they would remain at the rest stop until a disposition could be made on their status by the Immigration District Director in Omaha - our boss. It was a foregone conclusion of what was going to happen - service of voluntary departure orders for them all. The investigators on this case got the affirmation of the leader of the group, thirty people in all, that they would remain in place until the district office made a decision on their case, which would be no later than the next morning at 8:00 a.m.

What a surprise awaited the investigators the next morning! Not only had everyone disappeared, but there was not a tire track to indicate anyone had been there. All that paperwork ended up in the trash basket. The next day we did find out that this troop of people had been stopped near Saint Louis, Missouri. No one knew if local immigration officers had been notified, but almost positively they were. We do know, though, that many people were probably bilked in some way or the other by them in their trip across the United States if they had not been personally deported.

Just to show our job was not always serious, one day our contact representative at the front counter called to say that he was sending a gentleman back to our office with a request. I don't know why the receptionist bothered us with this guy, but anyway, here he came. I had him have a seat and asked him how I could help him, not knowing that he wasn't playing with a full deck. It didn't take me long though to see that his rambling prattle nailed him as a street person with an addled brain from too much cheap wine. Particularly when he told me that he was born on "The Easter Sunday in Golgatha." He obviously was alluding to the fact that he was Jesus Christ and born where Jesus was crucified - without all the facts straight. Catering to his request for a picture identification card, I told him that I would contact him when it was ready as I showed him the door. Fortunately, I never saw him again. I ask the contact representative to be more selective when he contacted our section.

Usually our marriage fraud investigations centered around Mexican males and United States citizen females duped into marriage and their filing spouse petitions for ultimate permanent residence to the U.S. This particular investigation involved a foreign student from Iran attending Drake University in Des Moines, Iowa, on the road to a degree as an osteopathic physician. On my request, they came to my office where I would separately interview them in order to obtain basic information about their marital relationship. Immediately after meeting them, I had a gut feeling that things were not copasetic. He was dressed in a suit and tie and had nicely coiffed hair; she was dressed for the occasion, however it was obvious that he outclassed her. His demeanor was of a person with a good education. She outweighed him by at least 50 pounds and her lack of education showed. Together they seemed congenial but their lack of personal interest in each other showed. After lengthy separate interviews, however, I found nothing disparately wrong.

After my interview with the couple, I made a visit to the petitioner's home and had a lengthy interview with the woman's parents. The father was older and unemployed. The home was neat and clean but apparently this family did not have much and it appeared as if they were receiving welfare. The dad and mother were gushy about the son-in-law; they had known him for some time and knew that he was a foreign student from Iran. All in all, he was the greatest and treated their daughter with the utmost love and affection. They said that he was a dedicated, hard-working student, and that he stayed there on weekends. He went to school in Des Moines, Iowa, some distance away. They both said that they had no doubts that there was mutual love between their daughter and son-in-law. Their daughter may have finished high school. I am not sure how it was related to me on how this couple met.

I was still bothered about this relationship. He certainly had reason to marry a U.S. citizen to gain permanent residence. For one thing, as a permanent resident his tuition to college would be considerable less. Their family backgrounds were miles apart. Culturally, educationally and religiously they did not match. I put a lot of time and effort on this matter and was reluctant to give my OK to adjudications on the spouse petition. I even held on to this case for some time hoping that I would get a different slant from either the in-laws or the petitioner. Finally, after much contemplation, I filed my report with everything that I had done. In my report I was adamant that consideration not be given for approval until the couple were again interviewed at least six months down the road. This did not happen! The beneficiary was given permanent residence. I never heard another word from the Examinations Unit.

"Now for the rest of the story," as Paul Harvey would say. About one year had passed when of all things; the American Consulate in Tehran, Iran sent a copy of a spouse petition to our office that the above Iranian had filed a spouse petition there for his Iranian wife. My suspicions were correct! So, I retraced my steps and again interviewed the parents and Iranian's previous Iowan wife.

Not surprisingly, the ex-wife told me in front of her parents, that this ex-husband of hers told her when they were on the way to my office in Omaha, "If you tell the immigration officer in Omaha anything negative about our relationship, I will kill you."

That seemed pretty strong wording. During questioning her about their divorce, she disclaimed knowing anything about it, and thought that the papers he had her to sign were school papers, even though their relationship went downhill shortly after their Omaha visit. The ex-in-laws then back-tracked their story when I told them of the divorce and of the illegal alien applying for an immigrant visa for his Iranian wife. All of a sudden, he was not as great as he originally turned out to be. Now they claimed when he did visit on weekends, he either slept in a tent in the back yard or on top of the covers when he slept with their daughter. Their previous effusiveness about how great the Iranian was now did a 180 turn! This family was completely hoodwinked by this individual. Sworn statements were taken as well, covering everything including the fact that the marriage had not been consummated. A subsequent rescission proceeding in Omaha to take the alien's permanent residence away was successful. He was deported to Iran. The petition he filed for his Iranian spouse in Tehran was denied. His name was placed in the Service lookout system. His medical education was disrupted in the U.S. I never heard from him again. Another poor girl was duped into marrying an alien for convenience. No showing of payment for this arrangement was established.

As it was, we investigators had plenty to do. However, we made time for ACIS, an acronym for Area Control Illegal Status, which meant seeking undocumented aliens (wetbacks) in either their work places or their temporary abodes. Packing plants and poultry processing plants maintained large work forces. Usually a large amount of the crews of such places harbored undocumented aliens, most of whom were from Mexico, but surprisingly we found numbers of aliens who had been admitted with valid passports and visitors' visas from underdeveloped European and African countries.

One packing plant in south Omaha, Cornhusker Pack, a privately-owned packing plant with a force of 200 or 300 individuals drew our attention one day in early 1976. I had presaged our visit with the owner, a Mr. Sherman. I had a long talk with him particularly in the inefficacy of hiring illegal aliens. Basing his operation on persons illegally in the U.S. would certainly be like a house of cards making no business sense. He, however, countered with the fact that Mexicans (wetbacks) were hard workers and could always be counted on. I also surmised that since it was not against the law to hire illegal aliens he always had a large contingent waiting at the door looking for work. Nevertheless, he consented to our checking his employees any time we wanted, and the best time to do so was at the morning break at 9:30 a.m. in the locker room. The only caveat; we were to tell him before we entered the locker room at the time or our arrival.

With four investigators, several sedans, two detention guards with vans and two ex-border patrolmen who were immigration examiners, we went to the Cornhusker Packing Plant. I led the entourage and was headed for Mr. Sherman's office to advise him of our intentions. However, before I was able to do so, the two ex-border patrolman, behind me, true to their spirit, viewed through the windows of the swinging doors into the plant proper, the kill floor and locker room, numerous persons of Mexican descent. They could not contain themselves and along with everyone else with us rushed through the swinging doors. Then all hell broke loose! Mr. Sherman ran out of his office screaming through a cigar he had in his mouth. "I told you to tell me before you came barging in," et cetera, et cetera. Trying my damndest to quiet him down and with little 'how do you do,' I joined the melee going on in the locker room.

The only way out of the lunchroom was through some swinging doors guarded by our entourage. Escape was fruitless! Before long, windows were broken for an escape route and humanity was swinging on overhead steam pipes, which were quickly broken with steam venting in all directions. It resembled an old Max Stennett movie picturing a Chinese fire drill. The workers on the kill floor were not represented, as they were about 30 minutes behind the mass of general workers, so they escaped. We rounded up over 25 undocumented Mexican males and then began our search of the lockers which yielded another dozen or so. These lockers were standard size: about 1 ½' X 1 ½' wide and deep and about 6' or so tall. All were made out of flimsy metal with legs that stood them about 6" off the floor. I opened one, and lo and behold it contained a Mexican male who soon disappeared from my direct sight when the bottom fell out of the locker. I said to the individual in Spanish, "?Que estas haciendo?" He replied in Spanish, "Cambiando mi ropa, no mas." I ask him, "What are you doing?" And he replied, "Changing my clothes, that's all." This warranted a big smile from me, as this worker fit firmly in the locker, with obviously no room to move about.

---

[15]Illegal Mexican aliens have been known to secret themselves in all kinds of strange places; the strangest place, a story relayed to me, was that an illegal alien in a packing plant in western Nebraska was found hiding in a vat of offal (guts) and breathing through a garden hose.

This particular operation at the Cornhusker Packing Company didn't seem to have a deleterious effect on my relationship with Mr. Sherman. I apologized profusely to him about our breach in the agreement with him, and after he cooled down, things remained cordial. I didn't report him to the ACLU as he could have had heartburn with this organization mainly due to the fact that he was definitely anti-black. If an African American applied for employment he had nothing available, but he was willing to hire the next Mexican who applied.

Another packing plant that particularly plagued us was just across the river in Council Bluffs, Iowa- American Beef Processors. They, like many of the others in that particular trade, needed workers and those workers translated into illegal Mexicans who were compliant, hard-working, uncomplaining and who had an incentive to work and send a good deal of their money back to their Mexican families. We would generally go unannounced to the front gate of American Beef and explain to the guard that we were there to check their personnel. It never failed, but each time we did this we were kept at the gate until the illegal Mexican population of the place could be hidden in various places in the plant. Since we hadn't come with warrants, that's what we had to contend with.

There are good times and bad times for the meat packing industry. For over a year American Beef closed shop during a down time in the industry. As times got better for the packing industry, American Beef Packing came under new management, and with that they were turning over a new leaf: From then on, hiring practices would change among other practices and they would hire through the local Department of Labor employment office instead of at the plant.

It was through this opportunity that the attorney for the company was contacted whereby I expressed our discontent of their previous hiring practices. It was unbelievable in our eyes what was happening at the company. I was assured that we could come any time to inspect their work force without delay at the front gate. It was not long after this meeting and after a briefing with the company supervisors concerning fraudulent documentation carried by illegal aliens that we got our first call of which we readily responded and made the apprehension of four Mexicans with "chueco," or fraudulent cards that were employment aspirants.

It didn't matter to us why or how we got cooperation form a meat packer. In this particular instance, American Beef Packing came under the auspices of the U.S. Department of Labor. It seems that company was being subsidized dollar for dollar for instituting a trainee program for butchers and packing house laborers. All that they had to do was show that they were complying with all the rules and regulations, and particularly not hiring illegal aliens. What a break for us. If only the other meat packers worked under such guidelines.

In the latter part of 1976 I met with the manager of a hide plant just south of Dakota City, Nebraska, at Sergeant's Bluff, and located near the Missouri river. The physical plant, a concrete block square constructed building, encompassed probably 5,000 to 8,000 square feet. One corner of the building held his office along with an open space with possibly 10 or 12 desks, separated by free standing dividers. The office space occupied the northwest part of the building, with large picture windows on the north and west side. I determined that around 35 or so workers were employed on the night shift, all of whom were probably undocumented Mexican males. The manager of the plant said have at it!

With two detention guards and their vans along with four of us investigators with two sedans we arrived at the front of the business around 7:00 p.m. The night shift supervisor greeted me as he ushered me into his office. Looking out his picture window and seeing the paucity of men and vehicles with me, he made the off-hand comment, "What are you going to do, surround this place?" knowing full well that we didn't have the man power to do so.

He took me to the swinging doors that opened up into the processing part of the plant. I was able to peer through the windowed doors and could make out an untold number of workers placing hides on a moving belt. The steam emanating throughout the area put a damper on the visibility. There was a considerable amount of noise coming from this work area. I was perplexed at how we were going to accomplish the task at hand of checking all these workers, when it came to me. I asked the supervisor to motion to the first worker on the chain that he was wanted on the telephone. And here came our first customer- I identified myself and asked him in Spanish, *"Dejeme ver por favor su identificacion para trabajando aqui en los Los Estados Unidos."* In English translation I was asking him for documentation that permitted him to work in the United States. Of course, as I expected, he was illegally here. I had him come with me and stand behind

---

[16] Phony or "chueco" cards were rampant in the early 70's. Nearly all illegal Mexicans carried one., usually in their socks. The most popular counterfeit was of the 1972 issue. For a trained eye they were easy to spot. The security punches and the A# was usually the give-away. In the 1960s such cards sold for as much as $500.00. Aliens were always admonished by the vendor not to show it to an immigration officer, but only to a prospective employer.

[17] An historic place on the Missouri River where Sergeant Floyd died of fever during the Lewis and Clark expedition in 1804.

a divider in the office. Believe it or not I was able to arrest at least 25 undocumented Mexican workers in this manner. As they came from the work area I had them stand behind office dividers - out of the sight of others. My cohorts waiting outside near our vehicles were dumbfounded when they saw workers piling up behind the dividers. The supervisor was incredulous that we didn't need to "surround the place." Soon we were processing aliens who subsequently were transported to Mexico. By the way, several got wind of my scheme and fled out the back way towards the Missouri river. Quite a number of the aliens possessed counterfeit alien cards that they had purchased in Los Angeles for various sums of money. These alien cards didn't pass muster by an immigration officer, but were used frequently to show employers as proof they were here legally.

One morning in in the fall of 1975, I had to return a call from the Douglas County Jail in Omaha concerning one of 'our' Nigerian foreign students who had been jailed on an assault charge; it seems that he slapped one of his countrymen in a fracas they had had.

I checked the jailee in our records and sure enough found him as having been admitted to attend John F. Kennedy College in Waterloo, Nebraska, and I hoofed down the jail to interview this detainee. Having no idea that he was out of status as a foreign student, but knowing full well that a good deal of them work without Service permission, I asked him point blank how long he had been working without authority (a minor assault charge usually would not affect a foreign student's status). After pondering the question a short moment he replied, "So that's how they want to play. I know a whole bunch of my so-called friends from Nigeria who are working without getting permission from the Immigration Service." It was hard to believe my ears when he rattled off names and places of employment of his 'so-called friends.' He even admitted to working as well as giving me the names of at least 25 of his cohorts. It looked like I had my work cut out for me.My investigation covered going to every place of employment of the Nigerian miscreants and getting dates, salary, length of employment, et cetera.

With this data in hand, I sent a call-in letter to every Nigerian that had been referred to me with specific interview dates and times that they were

---

[18]John F. Kennedy college was founded in 1969 in Wahoo, Nebraska, one of six colleges started by small town businessmen in the model of Parson College in Fairfield, Iowa. Due to a drop in enrollment and financial difficulties following the end of the draft in 1973, Kennedy College closed down in 1975.

[19]When aliens have the same deportation charge judges request that more than one at a time be tried. Five at a time before this particular judge were "mashed."

see me. As the foreign students met their dates and times in my office, I obtained data that would eventually lead to a hearing before an immigration judge. I presented each and every one of them an order to show cause as to why they should not be deported with exact dates and the times that they were meet the immigration judge. Since each of the Nigerian foreign students violated the terms of their admission by working without Service permission, and there were so many, we "mashed" their hearings. The judge in each and every one of these cases determined their deportability and they each were given the opportunity to leave the United States voluntarily. If they did not leave as directed they would then be deported at government expense. Voluntary departure would permit their future entry into the United States without seeking prior permission.

When I would pursue my investigative endeavors through Iowa it would usually be scheduled for a Monday through Friday. I would always have with me enough work to keep me busy during this time and to fill in I would take with me search leads to fill in my time in case in a particular area I had a time gap. This particular time I was traveling through Tama, Iowa, a small town in central Iowa, about 30 miles south and east of Marshalltown and about 75 miles from Des Moines, Iowa. The search lead that I had was a name and Tama address of a Polish individual in his early thirties, who entered the Polish ship, at Detroit, Michigan. There was no evidence that he had ever departed the United States.

I called on the address given on the search lead. It just happened to be one of the nicest homes in Tama- a white columned, two-story home that definitely stood out among the other homes in the area. The small Tama municipality was in the center of agriculture, an area where most everyone gained their living in that field. When I knocked on the door of this quite splendid home, a elderly gentleman in his sixties appeared to whom I identified myself, asking him if he knew this particular individual on whom I had the information. Looking rather disinterested, he advised me that he had never heard of the man and certainly could not explain why his residence had been given as a reference. He did politely tell me that if he came across this individual he would be sure to call me at the number on my calling card. He appeared less than interested.

Not giving up on my quest, knowing that somehow there was a reason for this guy's involvement in the whereabouts of my Polish alien, so I went

---

[20]The plant was originally built in 1971 and has operated under several owners. It shut down in 2001 after a mad cow scare led to a cutoff in U.S. exports. The plant employed up to 600 employees.

to the local post office and queried the clerk at the counter and asked him the same question about my Polish national. "Yes, I know that man, and at least seventy just like him. They even built a dormitory on the Tama Packing Company property," as he pointed up the hill from the post office. Now I had a good idea of where my Polish subject was, along with a great number of his ilk.

In early September or October 1976 I contacted the District Office about my discovery of this vast amount of what appeared to be Polish nationals who had entered the United States as visitors and who immediately went to work without the proper documentation. This obviously wasn't an opportune time to take advantage of this situation, and so I was advised to back off and wait until later in the year when we could get proper warrants and gather our resources to visit the "dormitory" en masse.

It wasn't a month later, probably in November, that we swooped down on this guesthouse of untold numbers of illegal aliens and made our play. We still didn't have more than half dozen officers and detention guards to "surround the place." Fortunately, there were not a lot of exits to the place. We started with a knock on the door. When a gentleman of unknown background answered the door, and obviously not Mexican, answered with the best English that he could muster and replied after we properly identified ourselves, "Passport Chicago." Before long, the company attorney arrived with an entourage including several English-speaking men who turned out to be permanent residents from Poland, and would be interpreting for us.

We had our bases covered and presented the warrants. The company attorney offered little resistance and stayed with us as the process of identifying and writing up what turned out to be at least seventy Polish males in their 20s and 30s. All had entered on the ship M/V Batory at the port of Detroit at various times, and had been working illegally for six months plus at this packing plant. Surprisingly, this large group of illegal's, gave us little trouble, and were amicable to work with - not like the other packing plants where the workers were extensively Mexican males.

However, several fled through the dark night out the back door or window of their quarters. One of my young compatriots took off after one who had fled the place, but within minutes was back in the residence, sans the escapee. Out of breath, he exclaimed, "I lost my handcuffs!" To which I replied, "How so?" Quickly retorting, he said, "I threw them at the sumbitch." I jokingly told him, "Next time don't let them have a head start."

The night of the "Poles" was long and tedious. The processing of this many certainly was a nerve-wracking job. We learned several things in our endeavors. The man in the large white, pillared house whom I had encountered a month or so ago that triggered this so-called "raid" was actually the superintendent of Tama Packing Company. There is a good chance he was correct in saying he didn't personally know the man I was looking for on the search lead. Helpful he was not! I am sure that he could have been more forthcoming and given me an earful about all the illegal aliens employed by his company. Also, we found out that one of our arrestees was a veterinarian in Poland, who earned more on the kill floor of this plant in a week than he did in a month in Poland and who had come to the United States to get a start in his career in Poland. Another worker was a degreed engineer who was making four times more in a week in this packing plant than he did in a month in his home country. This of course, was the largest contingent of non-Mexicans encountered and arrested at any given packing plant in the venue of Iowa and Nebraska.

We were unable to establish collusion by the company and all these illegal's, so prosecution of the establishment was denied. However, we announced to this more than helpful group through several interpreters that a decision would need to be made through the District Director early the next day concerning the disposition of all the immigration violators. We would need their solemn oath that they would not try to evade or leave the area until had a disposition on their cases. Without this assurance from them they would be locked up in the nearest jail in Marshalltown. We promised them that we would return by 8:00 a.m. the next morning.

We could not believe our eyes when we arrived at this barracks of meat-packing workers early the next morning. Spread out before us on several tables in this dining room of sorts was the most sumptuous feast one could imagine. Before us was Polish ham, salads of all sorts, desserts, etcetera. There was even cognac, vodka, and hard liquor. Their spokesman for the group through an interpreter thanked us greatly, and particularly since we had trusted them so much that we did not jail them all. We respectfully declined the "hard stuff" since we were working, but we dove in on the scrumptious pot luck spread before us. Winding up the affair, we were sung their rendition of the Polish national anthem, and of course we all partook in the Star Spangled Banner.

It was a memorable send-off that these Polish nationals received later on in the morning, each one having received official notification that they were given voluntary departure to depart for their home country within 30 days.[21] An extra section of the Greyhound Bus arrived near the downtown area of

---

[21] We had already decided that this would not be an option, but they had not been apprised of this.

town, and as these men boarded the buses dozens of people, mostly young females, crying, yelling and vowing their love and otherwise making themselves known. The plant did not open for several days due to the depletion of their work force. At least seventy positions were opened at the plant for native workers who were eligible to work.

These Polish nationals that we arrested had received their 5-year visitor's visas from Embassies in Krakow and Warsaw. I wonder what criteria the visa sections used to issue these visas? I prepared a memorandum through the District Director in Omaha outlining the details of this operation and my concerns about the legitimacy of the visas that had been issued to them. It was my hope that the information would be of use to the Embassies in future visa issuance, voicing my concern of how employable-age males could afford extended vacations in the United States, leaving families and work in their home country.

On my future visits to Iowa I always made it a point to hit the Tama Packing Plant to keep them honest. It looked like Operation Cooperation worked. I would always get a look at the new hires paperwork, and only a few times did I find a few Mexicans with counterfeit alien registration cards, who went back with me to Omaha for subsequent removal to Mexico.

Interestingly, this incident involving so many Polish nationals was almost like déjà vu for me. Nearly 10 years ago, when I was a young inspector at the border port of Morgan, Montana, a deluge of Polish nationals came to my attention in my stand-by work that I was serving for Chicago, when on several occasions I was sent extension work to be completed that included Polish men in employable ages of early 20s to middle 30s who had arrived in Detroit on the ship M/V Batory. They had all been admitted "face to face" by a U.S. Immigration Officer for periods of nomore that 2 weeks; almost immediately their travel agency put in for 6 month extensions. I bundled all these extension applications up, and for which I appended a memorandum explaining my doubts of the legitimacy of such requests. It didn't take a brain surgeon to question how these individuals could afford such an extended vacation. A humble immigration officer could hardly handle financially more than two week's vacation. I never heard from the Chicago office on this matter but I never received that type of extension work again.

Sioux City, Iowa was one of our prime work spots involving marriages of convenience and the large numbers of Mexican male southern border jumpers working in and around the city and across the Missouri River in Dakota City, Nebraska and the environs. One of my favorite law enforcement officers was Alan Blythe, sheriff, with his office and jail in Dakota City,

Nebraska. We housed a number of our detainees in his jail. He always treated us with respect and he welcomed us on our trips to Dakota City, Nebraska. We jokingly called him the only law west of the Missouri River. He was a strict law enforcement officer and took his job seriously. He was dead set against violators of the law, no matter if they were Mexicans guilty of a misdemeanor classified as a petty offense. It's hard to believe, but despite the pace maker he had implanted, he could outrun any of us in a foot race after an illegal alien. He was always eager to assist us in our "raids."

One particular event that we participated in in his territory involved so many illegal Mexican aliens that we chartered a Greyhound bus. We had around sixty or sixty-five detainees in his jail. This particular Fall day we had footraces after a number of Mexicans. Having a number in custody, we looked awe-stricken seeing Alan Blythe chasing a miscreant across a plowed field and his ultimately proud look with a cuffed alien in his custody. Most of the aliens had been working at the local Iowa Beef Processing (IBP) plant, which on a good day would kill over 2000 head of cattle, that would have come from feed lots all over the Midwest. Stockyards in Omaha, Sioux City, Chicago et cetera were of the past. Also, the days of shipping hanging beef was a thing of the past. IBP was the innovator of boxing prime cuts of beef and shipping them across the United States in large semi trucks. There was a tremendous need for butcher help and a good number of illegal Mexicans filled the bill.

Usually, the Government would normally foot the bill for the chartered bus. I was determined, though, that these fence jumpers should pay their share of transportation back to Mexico, the only punishment they would get for entering the country illegally. We had a van with us that day and I escorted our driver/guard to the drive-in of the local bank with several loads and explained to an officer of the bank what we had- a bus full of illegal aliens with little identification and their pay checks. Asking him as a concerned citizen if he could see fit to cash their checks so that they could pay for their lift back to Mexico. It was no sweat! That bus ended up costing us very little.

By the time the bus got underway, numerous cars packed with females crowded the street near the jail. Most of these enamored females had boyfriends who had been arrested and were screaming and hollering to their loved ones, "Don't forget me, I love you, see you soon," and other terms of endearment. Believe it or not, many of the arrestees could not have been less interested, and in fact, a number of them gave the impression that they were glad to be rid of their "so-called" girlfriends. We were mistaken when we thought we had seen the last of the carloads of women. Keeping ahead of the bus, they stopped several times on the interstate, ahead of the bus, waving, throwing kisses and screaming terms of endearment as the bus flew by. Finally, the farewell raucous was over and the Mexican men, safely ensconced in their bus seats and guarded by a detention guard, settled back to await their arrival at the Texas/Mexico border later the next day.

IBP for a long time had been on our short list to check their employees in the company lunch room. Having become acquainted with the head of security at the plant, an ex-FBI agent, the guy was in every way cooperative and even encouraged us to perform our duties as we saw fit. The particular night in question that we had set for the so-called "raid," our group of investigators and detention guards were settled in my room at the local Holiday Day Inn in Sioux city awaiting a call from security at IBP for the go-ahead. When the phone rang, anxious for the moment to go, were disheartened when we got the word from head of security let the wind out of our sails. "Sorry fellows, but I don't think it would be a good time for you guys to show up. One of our Mexican clean-up crew was killed when he fell into a meat grinder that had been inadvertently turned on." Naturally, we all were affected in a bad way, and not because we were raring to go either. Later our operations were successful enough in the Sioux City area just checking the numerous scabby apartments Mexican line jumpers inhabited.

Some time before I had introduced myself to the Chief of the Sioux City, Iowa police department and I had made friends with a number of policemen. One particular night, the Chief explained to me that they were going to set up a routine traffic check on the Sioux City, Iowa side of the Missouri River as the shift let out at the IBP Plant and I was invited along. He assured me that it would be mostly Mexican males, status in the United States undetermined that would be encountered. Sure enough, he was right! Each car held about four males, Mexican descent. Looking over the patrolman's shoulder I could see the driver's license and other identification proffered by each of the occupants. What a night it turned out to be! I made no motion, just observed when ID was presented. There was a goodly amount of counterfeit alien registration cards, and some who could not speak English. That night was quite productive with more than a score who were arrested by me and the police had a field day too with unlicensed drivers, traffic wants, etcetera.

One evening I made a house call on a purported marriage of "good faith" in one of the more run-down sections of Sioux City. As much as I hate to admit, I am without doubt sure that this city has never, ever received a "city of the year award." Parts of Sioux City at one time must have enjoyed a more prosperous era. In fact, you could see that the home that I approached had one time many years before enjoyed an elite status. Now though, the place had been broken up into a number of apartments that were run-down. I was looking for a particular couple who allegedly lived there.

I knocked on the first door just inside the front of the building. When the door opened I could hardly believe my eyes! The front room of this once elegant building contained a room full of Mexican males. Very quickly I could see that discretion was the better part of valor, and there was no way I could single-handedly arrest all those who came into view. I professed to the fellow answering the door that I was a salesman pursuing my trade. With that he closed the door, apparently not aware that I was an investigator for Immigration Service, and not wanting what I was selling. I backtracked to my vehicle and contacted my buddies at the Sioux City Police Department, asking for a back up and paddy wagon. Within just a very short while there came three or four black and whites and a paddy wagon. With my reinforcements to cover my back, we retraced my steps to the what appeared to be an overloaded apartment. The catch that night was over twenty-five illegal Mexican males, which kept me occupied with paper work for some time. I appropriately thanked the Chief of Police and all the officers who assisted me that night.

The officers of the Sioux City, Iowa policemen were dedicated in whatever law enforcement activity they were involved with. For that reason, I always stopped by the station and made my presence known. Oftentimes they gave me information on persons they had questioned and had produced what appeared to them as "phony" alien cards. With an address in hand, I was usually successful in arresting at least one who would also show me the same "phony" card. My association with this group of dedicated officers made my job a lot more productive.

It was enjoyment apprehending illegal aliens and making room in the work force for United States citizens and aliens lawfully in this country. But every time I drove north on Interstate 29 approaching Sioux City, there was an obnoxious smelling rendering plant on the east side of the highway. The foul aroma and stench emanating from this place was gut wrenching to say the least and I am sure that it did not enhance the air quality in that part of Sioux City. I swore that if ever I received a complaint of illegal alien(s) working at that place they could stay there. Do you know what? No one ever complained.

On a monthly basis the immigration judge headquartered in Denver visited Omaha to conduct exclusion, deportation and rescission hearings. On his road trip to started in Kansas City, Missouri, then to Saint Louis, Missouri and lastly Omaha. We had a full slate for him which normally took two days. Since our Service did not see fit to assign a Trial Attorney to travel with the judge, myself and another investigator served as acting Trial Attorneys to act as the government advocate on the monthly trips the judge made to Omaha. In the capacity of the acting Trial Attorney, my responsibility was to make sure that all paper work had been prepared correctly and supporting documentation was at hand to support charges outlined in the order to show cause. During the hearing process for exclusion and deportation, a civil process is begun with an explanation by the judge to the respondent about the trial (in a criminal trial the person being tried is called the defendant). Then he/she is asked if they have representation - at least half of the respondents do not have an attorney. In other words they acted Pro Se. None will be appointed by the court, and in most cases which are single irrefutable charges against the individual - for example, overstaying admission, illegal entry, working without Service permission, can be handled without an attorney.

Also explained to the respondent is the nature of the proceedings. Determination of excludability or deportation is the first and important part of the hearing process. The hearing process is bifurcated, meaning that if the charge is sustained the second part of the whole procedure will then center on whether the judge will invoke the rule as to how and when the individual must leave the country. A good attorney hired by the respondent could plea for a longer period of time, giving reasons therefore, or humanitarian reasons against deportation. At this point in the hearing process, the judge will make his decision as to the how and when or whether the individual is eligible for relief from actual deportation. Acting in behalf of the government, the trial attorney raises any issues that may contradict the how or when of voluntary departure and recommendation for deportation and the reasons therefore.

In my experience as Acting Trial Attorney one hearing of particular note was at the prison in Anamosa, Iowa. The respondent in this particular case was a Mexican male, in his late 30s who had been illegally in this country since his elementary school days. He had been in and out of a number of foster homes and had led a troubled life. He had long ago lost contact with his mother and father and knew of no siblings. He had a long juvenile record, and had spent most of his adult life in prison. There appeared to be no doubt about the fact that he was incorrigible and that he had no claim on United States citizenship or legal status in the United States.

It was very difficult to even look squarely at the individual. His face was horribly disfigured, having wrapped himself in toilet tissue some time before and set himself on fire. The individual seemed to understand the charges but he was basically indifferent to the whole thing. He did not refute anything. The judge found him deportable and entered an order of deportation. As the government's representative I could see no sense for amelioration of the charges. This was a sad, sad case. This hideous looking individual had a number of years on his prison sentence to go. I placed an immigration hold on this guy, in the eventuality of sometime in the future his being released. There is no doubt he was going to have a rough time of it. By this time he may have committed suicide.

The most satisfying time that I spent as Acting Trial Attorney was when I represented the government at the rescission hearing that involved a fraudulent marriage between an Iranian student from Des Moines, Iowa who duped a young woman and her family into thinking how great he was. The gratifying thing about this was that I did the original marriage investigation and I finally got him! In the culmination of my investigation I was not reconciled to the fact that the marriage was valid and recommended that before the alien was issued an alien card for permanent residence that the case would be reopened and the couple would be re-interviewed. It did not happen!

Through this fraud marriage he obtained permanent residence; through subterfuge he tricked this young woman into signing divorce papers - she allegedly said that she thought the papers she had signed were something to do with school. I truly think that she was looking for a better station in life. Within a year this guy was back in Iran and filed a spouse petition for his Iranian wife. Before he could get his Iranian wife to the United States he was brought before an Immigration Judge in Omaha in proceedings that would take away his permanent residence. Before the judge ruled definitively on this case he went or fled to Iran. Arrangements were put in place to keep him from returning to the United States. Finally, justice was served!

One of the last hearings that I was involved with as acting Trial Attorney in Omaha was the hearing of the twenty-five or so Nigerian ex-students from John F. Kennedy College in Wahoo, Nebraska. In 1975 the college went bankrupt and left a student body of more than 800 in the lurch, which included these Nigerian students. When the college left them high and dry they scattered to the four winds; most of them however, remained in Nebraska, seeking work where ever they could find it. This did not make them less amenable to deportation. Discussing this issue before, they were all issued orders to show cause why they should not be deported which culminated in the immigration judge found them all deportable as charged. At the hearing none of them denied having violated their immigration status, and admitted to the charges against them. As the acting Trial Attorney I proffered all the evidence that I had gathered concerning their violation of status. When the judge came to the manner of their departure I was not against them being granted a definite time for which them to depart the country voluntarily. In the alternative, if they failed to depart in a timely manner they were to be taken into custody and physically deported from the United States.

A strange thing did happen involving a Nigerian at a hearing in which I was acting Trial Attorney. Most were in "mashed" hearings because of the same charges. This one, however, was separate for some reason. After the judge had read the charges and asked the respondent how he pled, instead of answering the question, and mind you this was being recorded, he quietly stated that he had turned to a friend of his who was married, and who was aware of the hearing, to ask him if he could borrow his wife to represent herself as his wife at the hearing, obviously making an attempt to ameliorate his "punishment" at the hearing. The judge looked at me and I at him quizzically, thinking to myself how stupid can you get? Obviously the guy was found deportable but not because he was a little "touched" in the head.

What a Pandora's Box I opened the day that I had set up all those out-of-status Nigerian students from John F. Kennedy College. I lost count of the number of quick marriages to United States citizens that precipitated fraud investigations from this episode. It is recalled that at least one of the Nigerians ended up doing hard time at the state prison in Lincoln, Nebraska on serious fraud charges.

On a winter evening in 1977 a colleague of mine, on-call, asked me to give him a hand concerning a call he had received from a concerned citizen in south Omaha. It seems that his sister lived in this particular block where there were also a considerable number of Mexican males, presumably all illegal, living in a run-down house that had been turned into apartments. It seemed that almost every time that his sister was on the street she would be accosted, pestered and otherwise bothered by different ones of these Mexican males.

While Patrolling Backwards

The night was quite dark, with no discernible moon light, when we were parked almost in front of this place where a considerable number of men boarded. I remember that there was no street light. Lights were visible in the apartment house, in fact three or four of the rooms had light. Knocking on the first door of the ante way a Mexican male answered. There were probably four or five men in the large bedroom/living area engrossed in television and playing cards. Quickly identifying ourselves, we soon had in our custody the men, all from Mexico, and who had entered the United States without documentation. Keeping our activities quiet so as not to disturb occupants of the other apartments we quietly took them to our van.

Going to the other apartments we encountered the same as the first. All in all we arrested around twenty Mexican males who had entered the United States like their friends. Putting the last of the Mexicans in the van two more walked up on the sidewalk, nearly running into us in the dark. In they went with the others. Naturally, we took them, one by one back to their hovels to get their stuff and furnished them with potato sacks to carry same. One young fellow, sort of ashamed to tell me, said that he had some Playboy magazines in his room hidden under his mattress that he wanted to be sure to get. He said that he didn't want the woman he rented from to think less highly of him for having them in his possession. We never heard from the informant again, so we must have solved his sister's problem.

In the summer of 1977, incarcerated in the local jail was a young almost handsome Mexican male of about 25 years of age. It escapes me now, but he was in jail for some petty offense and he was being held for us as an illegal Mexican alien. He was a really likeable kind of a guy, and spoke almost impeccable English. I don't know whether he had attained his English fluency during a lengthy stay in the United States, or whether he gained proficiency in English working as he had told me in resorts in Acapulco. Nevertheless, he had employment in Waterloo and had been here long enough to get himself a girlfriend. Apparently, she had visited him several times during his jail tenure, and at the same time his male friend, a United States citizen, came to the jail, oddly enough, when his girl friend visited him. Handcuffed, we headed for my car at which time, (he was always very polite to me), he asked in his almost flawless English the favor of going by this girl friend's apartment to say goodbye.

Parking the car at the apartment, I could see that he was becoming uneasy, but he didn't say anything. His hands were handcuffed in front, as I didn't feel that in the back was necessary. After three or four steps we were in the apartment- his girlfriend's door was on the left. He immediately started pounding on the door with his manacled hands and very shortly his girl friend opened the door, dressed in a bathrobe. I found out quickly that

83

something was askance, particularly when he pushed himself into the bedroom. Lo and behold! There lay his good friend in the bed from which the girlfriend had arisen. There were a lot of tears from my handcuffed Mexican friend and a lot of excuses from his girlfriend that were not making a lot of sense. His male friend got out of the trysting bed and headed into the kitchen for a drink. He was cornered as the Mexican lad approached him, hitting him with his handcuffed hands first one side then the other. The philanderer did not make an effort to protect himself, probably knowing that he had it coming. The girlfriend was then crying and still making excuses. Apparently she wasn't as head over heels in love with my Mexican companion as he thought.

My Mexican detainee looked at me and said, "We can go now, Mr. Hattery." We were parked next to his friend's car, which he originally saw, igniting his uneasiness. Just before he climbed into the back seat of the government car, he gave several resounding revengeful kicks to his ex-buddy's car. I made no comment to the individual I had in custody about either act. As far as I was concerned the two-timing "friend" had it coming.

Surprise of all surprises! The supervisory Inspector In-Charge at Blaine, Washington found another assignment to add to his resume: Mexico City, Mexico, where he would be charged with field investigations and other immigration-related work out of the Embassy. (He was a climber, concluding his career as Chief Patrol Agent in New Orleans, Louisiana upon retirement) The position in Blaine that he had held for around two years was now vacant. To make a long story short, I was selected for the job. The guy I was replacing I had known for almost ten years, as a fellow-student in attendance at the journeyman school in Port Isabel, Texas.

It looked as though this was my "Swan Song" as an a criminal investigator in Omaha, Nebraska. I can say quite easily that my stint as criminal investigator of nearly five years was the most challenging, most varied, and most time-consuming of anything I had done in the Service. What a place to learn everything there is to know about one's job, and what a satisfying job. Being solely responsible for one's own activities and not knowing what the next day would bring was an indescribable opportunity.

Unfortunately for me, though, I never had the privilege of attending basic investigators' school. Shortly after my arrival at Omaha, the investigator who showed me the ropes was to attend investigators' school. And, about a year later, a new investigator on board and I, as an old hand got the nod for school. The two short courses that I took were a local week course on technical report writing, and I can't complain about this one: EEO Investigators School at New Orleans, Louisiana for two weeks. I couldn't complain, though!

Supervisory Inspector In-Charge

I was welcomed by telephone to the Seattle District, by Joseph Swing, Jr. District Director upon my arrival at Blaine. He was quite congenial and definitely not dictatorial. Mr. Swing would be in place for several years before his retirement in the mid 1980s. Directly under him on the organizational chart was the Assistant District Director for Examinations, to whom I reported directly. Director Swing started his career in the State Department, switching over to the Immigration Service, then rising rather quickly through the ranks. I have no doubts that his rabbi was his father (see footnote).

At this juncture of my career I felt at ease, competent and comfortable. I already knew beforehand that this position would be unlike anything I had done before - certainly not as exciting as my previous assignment in investigations. Now I would be responsible for the work of others, also unlike anything that I had to do before. My patience would be tried; there would be times of grief and also, joy. It took me a while to learn that by sleeping on a problem, perceived difficulties weren't so problematical after all.

Having spent from October 1970 to January 1974 at Blaine previously as an inspector had made coming back as "old home week". Many of our friends and my co-workers welcomed us back. Three of the inspectors I had worked with before had been promoted and would be my subordinate supervisory staff. I was glad-handed by two of them; in fact, one had called me when he heard that I had been promoted to congratulate me. The one supervisor who was not so happy felt that he should have been selected for the vacancy, and until his retirement several years away he showed his disenchantment.

Upon my arrival at Blaine, we had a staff of about 35, three of whom were supervisors, one administrative clerk and the rest were inspectors carrying with them various amounts of experience and education. With this cadre of officers 24/7 coverage was maintained. We shared traffic lane responsibilities equally with our sister agency, U.S. Customs. At the time, my agency was under the Justice Department and U.S. Customs was under

---

[22]Position was up graded to GS/GM 13 w/title Port Director in 1980s.
[23]District Director Swing's father, Joseph May Swing (2/28/1894- 12/9/1984) was a retired Lieutenant general in the army a protégé of Eisenhower , and the Commissioner of Immigration in the 1950s. He was responsible for a huge roundup of illegal Mexicans in south Texas during his tenure, which prompted posted signs: "We don't serve Border Patrolmen or Niggers.."

the Treasury Department. We were out-manned three to one by Customs. Later on I acquired a framed satirical depiction by the famous cartoonist, Jimmy Hatlo, with his "Tip of the old Hatlo Hat" showing several immigration officers working their tails off at the counter and in the background four or five Customs officers, feet propped on desks, doing nothing but twiddling their fingers. This framed cartoon decorated my office wall during the years of my employment at Blaine. Obviously, there was general knowledge of our ration of inspectors.

All three of my supervisors were military veterans with Border Patrol backgrounds and probably averaged over 15 years of experience. One of them had been a guard at Alcatraz before entering the Immigration Service and one had been a Naval Corpsman in World War II. They all proved to be exemplary supervisors.

Six of my inspections staff to be were recent graduates of IOBTC (Immigration Officers Basic Training) and all of whom were previous Justice Department employees. Several of them were radio operators (experience carried over from their military days) and detention guards, et cetera. All but one of these officers have long since retired. The lone man, now with nearly 35 years service to his credit is a supervisory inspector with his nose still to the "grindstone."

I eventually selected on reassignments at least three officers who wanted to get away from the southern border as Border Patrolmen. They made great inspectors and carried with them a certain enforcement mode. Alas, being locked into a particular place
such as traffic inspections prevailing, they eventually returned to their first love: U.S. Border Patrol, an on-your-own, less constricting pursuit.

One particular officer, who had "washed out" of the Border Patrol but picked up as a detention guard, was able to get his foot in the door again by being selected as a trainee immigration inspector. Successfully completing his basic training he was selected as a trainee at Blaine. He was a sharp individual, single, tailored uniforms fine representative of the Service and all. After several years of completion as a journeyman officer, an opening came up in the Blaine Sector for a journeyman Border Patrolman, which would have been a lateral transfer. The only kicker to this was that there needed to be a certification of Spanish fluency by his supervisor. He came to me for the certification. When he had washed out of the Border Patrol Academy his problem was his lack proficiency in Spanish. Sadly enough, he had done nothing in the four or five years since he had left the Patrol to acquire proficiency in Spanish. As I had explained to him, I was unable to provide the necessary certification because of that. I am sure that he would have been a "shoo-in" for the job in the Patrol. An excellent appraisal would have preceded him, and I certainly would have been on his band-wagon. He did well as an immigration inspector up until the day of his retirement. A new facility was built at the Pacific Highway (commonly known as the truck customs) with a larger truck inspection facility, classification & value section and three covered lanes (not high enough for a motor home w/air conditioner unit on top) for autos and non-commercial vehicles. Also included was an up-to-date bus inspection facility. A large one-story building adjacent to the traffic lanes was used communally by Immigration, Customs and Agriculture for inside business. The completion date of this facility was 1977. My office was temporarily in the north end of the building during the construction phase of the two-storied facility at the Peace Arch. There was under cover parking for secondary inspections with about twenty parking slots. The facility had traffic lanes on either side of the building, three covered and one uncovered on the west side of the building and four traffic lanes on the east for over-flow traffic on weekends and holidays. Again, the covered inspection lanes would not permit a motor home with an air conditioning unit on top. The downstairs of this building was also communal: one half of the front counter inside was devoted to Immigration and the other half to Customs. About one half of the downstairs was allotted to Customs and the other half to Immigration referral matters.

Spending about one year in my spacious office at the Pacific Highway during the construction phase that was completed in the fall of 1978 at the Peace Arch, I looked forward to moving into my permanent office on the second floor of the building, which overlooked Peace Arch Park on the north and Georgia Strait on the west, with Blaine Marina with its innumerable boats of all sizes and descriptions. We worked out of a double-wide trailer while the new Peace Arch was under construction. Only two lanes for traffic prevailed at the Peace Arch, which lent a natural tendency for knowable, local dwelling people to use the new Pacific Highway crossing

---

[24]Wikipedia, the free encyclopedia, lends this description of the Peace Arch: Park and environs: The Peace Arch Park consists of Peace Arch Provincial Park on the Canadian side and Peace Arch State Park on the American side of the border. Within the park I a major border crossing (between Interstate 5 on the U.S. side and British Columbia Highway 99 on the Canadian side) which has never closed, symbolizing a long history of peace between the two nations. In Canada, the crossing is officially named Douglas in honor of Sir James Douglas, the first governor of the Colony of British Columbia. Because of the Peace Arch monument, however, the border crossing between Surrey and Blaine is popularly known as the "Peace Arch Border Crossing", one of the busiest border crossings between Canada and the United States. It is the busiest such crossing west of Detroit.

to avoid traffic-tie ups.

The Peace Arch Inspection facility meant the combination of the actual location of the Peace Arch station adjacent to the actual park, named the Peace Arch, and mutually taken care of by the State of Washington and British Columbia, Canada. The truck customs approximately one mile east, titled locally as the truck customs (obviously, immigration work was conducted there also. Highway 99 in British Columbia meets Interstate I-5 at the Peace Arch. Highway 15 (or 176th Avenue) in British Columbia meets State Route 543 at the truck route (Pacific Highway crossing northbound).

The motto I felt apropos was what I learned in journeyman school eight years previously, "Look Good, Talk Nice, and Use Good Judgment." That would be our motto during my tenure. I impressed upon my subordinate supervisors that as ambassadors of the United States, so to speak, we were to look and act like professionals. Many of the people we would encounter in our official capacity would be a first time visitor to the United States; therefore our best comportment would be expected.

Since I had been an immigrant inspector for nearly eight years, I was particularly concerned about the safety, health and comfort of the officers when they were assigned outside traffic. When the work was completed at both the Peace Arch and Pacific Highway ports of entry, the inspection booths were equipped with full-length sliding doors on two sides. The air quality at and near the booths was to say the least, poor. It was my contention that the booths should be retro-fitted with Dutch doors. With the full-length doors open, autos passing through the traffic lane would spew nauseous gas fumes into the booth, making a serious health problem for the inspectors.

Approaching our Regional Office with a memorandum outlining the poor air quality surrounding the booths and how the issue could be addressed with the placement of Dutch doors, I was rebuffed. In a rather terse reply to my inquiry, it was stated that it was felt that the quality of inspections would suffer, as the officers were less apt to properly inspect incoming traffic. I never bothered to reply. It was my opinion that there would always be a few officers who would tend to remain seated, but the majority would do a good job, especially if they knew we were looking out for their health.

Undaunted, I discussed the door issue with the head custodial guy at GSA (Government Services Administration) locally. They had already made air studies in the traffic inspection areas and found the quality of air poor to miserable. No sweat! I was assured that they would run with the ball and retrofit all the inspection booths with Dutch doors. Guess what...all of the border inspection facilities in Washington State have been replaced over the years and have been outfitted with Dutch doors. Nary a word of this got to our Regional Office. Only my subordinate supervisors were made aware of my Dutch door caper. For the inspectors, it was just business as usual. By the way, nowadays (thirty years hence) the booths are really comfortable with air-conditioning, heated inside and outside, communication to inside and other booths, and radio contact with Border Patrol for run-throughs and computerization through and through. And to think that for years inspection booths were unheard of!

On May 24, 1979 at the lazy laid-back port-of-entry Lynden, Washington a shooting tragedy occurred, less than year since my entry on duty at Blaine. At the port-of-entry, about fifteen miles from Blaine, a good friend of my mine who was a full-time school teacher and a part-time immigration inspector was on duty. Only one other officer was working that day and had his turn inside. He was Customs Inspector Kenneth G. Ward. The Immigration officer, whom I had known for years, was unarmed and was working traffic out of a make shift inspection booth. Artie Ray Baker and his girl friend drove up. Suspecting something was not kosher sent them both inside for an in-depth pat-down, "take everything out of your pockets" type of a deal. The next thing my friend heard was several shots inside and momentarily shots rang out as the couple headed out the door of the facility, firing and missing at my friend by inches, one round going into the booth and one round into the Canada Customs building. How this couple got into Canada is unknown, but Baker had escaped from a prison camp in California where he had been prosecuted for murder. The couple fled the area in their car, but were captured less than 24 hours later when they abandoned their conveyance on the Nooksack River.

The investigation that ensued revealed that when Baker and his girlfriend were sent inside, the Customs officer had Baker and his girlfriend take out everything out of their pockets. After the Customs officer checked their IDs in the next room and as he approached the couple, Baker pulled a semi automatic .45 caliber gun from his belt in back and fired point-blank into the Custom officer's face. In their flight out the front door, Baker's girlfriend pulled the door forcefully against the lifeless body of the slain officer on the floor. Obviously, if my friend had been armed he could not have saved his partner; he would have been able to protect himself though and

---

[25]Customs officers had been required to be armed for a number of years. This tragedy gave impetus to the formalization of requirements for Immigration Inspectors to carry a weapon. Up to this point quarterly pistol qualifications were mandated, but pistol carrying was not. For a full depiction of this tragedy go to Google on the internet and type in Kenneth G. Ward.

possibly have stopped the shooter's flight.

Never in my nearly 20 years experience at the time had I encountered such a travesty so close to home and to someone I knew so well. There is an abject lesson here. An officer working inspections traffic has one of the most dangerous jobs there is. An inspector is not prescient enough to know that the next vehicle driving up could spawn a situation such as this one depicted. These incidents obviously can even be few and far between.

In the absence of a firearms officer, several times over the years at Blaine I personally conducted quarterly firearms instruction. Upon my arrival in Blaine in 1978 we had an arsenal of four or five .38 caliber heavy (blunderbuss) revolvers that we signed out to officers on a shift basis. In light of what happened at Lynden, officers became more aware of the dangers of the job and eventually it was mandated that all officers would qualify on a quarterly basis by a qualified firearms instructor and were issued top-of-the line semi-automatic weapons. Our Service was so serious about the gun issue that if one had not been through the Border Patrol Academy or had graduated from Immigration Officers' Basic Training courses where gun training/qualification was mandatory they had to attend the Academy. Eventually, a subordinate supervisor of mine had to attend the Academy, where he audited everything but firearms instruction. The Port Director at Sumas, nearing retirement, had never even attended the Border Patrol Academy nor had he ever had any formal firearms training by a qualified academy-trained instructor. He kept his fingers crossed and was able to retire before he had to attend the Academy.

It is hard to conceive, but our Canadian counterparts were not sufficiently convinced that the killing of our border officer was enough cause to consider arming their officers. It has been only since 9/11 and the bombing of the World Trade Towers in New York City that our Canadian colleagues seriously thought of arming their officers. Several times in the last few years, Canadian inspectors have abandoned their posts when advised of the possible approach of an armed and dangerous suspect, only returning to their posts when everything was "safe." At last reports (thirty-two years after the Lynden POE shooting) progress is being made in arming their officers. Believe it or not, even though we had body armor furnished, only a few officers elected to wear it, even in light of the Lynden incident. Customs never had body armor to wear, but one of them came to me one day to ask for it to be issued for him. Without hesitation, I had him sign for it.

Shortly after the Lynden travesty (which now is the Kenneth G. Ward Port of Entry) and mop up work was being done after we had moved in at the Peace Arch, a terrible incident confronted us. In my office in the early spring of 1979, I was buzzed on my intercom from downstairs and I was told that a little girl had been hit by a pickup truck in the parking area on the east side of the building, 911 had been called and they were on their way.

When I got to the outside of the building, emergency medical personnel, firemen and policemen were on the scene and several of them had already begun working on the frail, limp little body. Minutes seemed like hours and they had not been successful in resuscitating her. Probably a good hour lapsed as they tried with all their might to save her. Every passing minute brought the recollection of seeing my 3 ½ year old son, lifeless on the street after he was hit by a car nearly fifteen years before.

After quite some time, I went with this Mexican family, who by the way had come from the American Consulate in Vancouver with their visas in hand for immigrating to the United States, to Saint Joseph's Hospital in Bellingham. There they were given the sad news that their 5-year old daughter had not made it. I gave this family as much consolation as I could muster in my distraught condition, gave them all a squeeze and departed. What a way to turn a day for these people from their happiness in finally getting permanent status in the United States into this tragedy! At this point in my career, in charge of immigration at Blaine, being beset with this tragedy was tough beyond imagination. I never had a premonition that incidents such as this would also happen. I have always wondered what happened to this family who had been stricken with such grief. That little girl would be over 32 years of age now.

More than several times early on my move to the Arch I had surprises awaiting me as I unlocked my office door. Under the door at different times notes in envelopes, sealed and unaddressed, had been placed. Two individuals had figured, I guess, that this was the manner in which to communicate with me, concerns they had informing me or some slight or action they wanted me to be aware of. The notes were always signed. It's anyone's guess why they contacted me in this way - perhaps because they got no satisfaction from their supervisors - or possibly, because I had been on a more personal basis with them before when I was an inspector at Blaine. Probably the latter was the reason.

One of the letters I recall was from one of the GSA employees listing mundane grievances such as rather silly occurrences of officers littering the inspection booth floors with peanut hulls, having firecrackers thrown at them, making skid marks on the floor during jumping contests, ad nauseam. Pretty tame stuff. My supervisors took care of this issue.

In another instance, the author of one of the letters, a Customs officer, complained to me that a certain inspector of mine used profanity as they were passing each other and calling him names, belittling his efforts as an inspector and belittling him. This I also passed along to one my supervisors. Obviously we had to get along. His one missive delivered to me under the door grabbed my attention immediately. It seems that an officer on my staff had pointed a gun at him, an antagonist who had been belligerent with him. This was a serious accusation. Feeling this issue needed more than a cursory examination, a call was placed to OPR (Office of Professional Responsibility) for their take after explaining the background. They too thought that this issue was serious, and would send an investigator to interview the informant.

In short span of several days two investigators arrived at my office to obtain first-hand knowledge of the gun incident. Of course, what I had was the letter of the informant. What they needed was a statement from the claimant. The guy was on days off, but lived only a short distance from the office when they appeared at this residence to get resolution of the matter in the form of a sworn statement. Rousing him at his door, they identified themselves giving reason for their appearance. Without as much as a sorry for inconveniencing them, he rebuffed them and refused to give them a statement.

Neither I nor investigations heard from this guy again. However, he became a thorn in the side of his Customs supervisors over a period of years. His personal complaint file grew to several inches in thickness, everything from injuring himself on the 'heavy' industrial doors, and other work-born injuries to justify his unusual use of sick leave, and of course, slights or confrontations with other officers. Anything and everything to justify his weirdness. He eventually was able to claim and was successful in obtaining some sort of a medical retirement. Poor guy! He didn't live long enough to enjoy his retirement. Maybe his tombstone should have read, "See I told you I was sick." In retrospect, those instances above were the only times that I received any mail under my door to call my attention to something that needed to be taken care of.

In early 1980 or 1981 I received a call from the District Director in Helena, Montana, a fine gentleman who was the Deputy District Director in Omaha when I worked there. They had just completed a deportation hearing that afternoon involving a female Canadian citizen married to a U.S. citizen. It was a "slam dunk" hearing; the female respondent had convictions for multiple narcotic-related crimes, et cetera, in which the judge ordered her deported forthwith under the custody of the Service. Her husband, with like convictions and a rap sheet a "mile long", was fortuitously born in the United States. He proclaimed in court, though, that he was going to kill an immigration officer due to his wife being deported. His spouse went one way and he the other. She was from British Columbia and there was a good chance he would be following her. However, he was not allowed in Canada, as he had been deported from that country.

If this guy were to carry out his death threat it could be in our neighborhood since his wife was from British Columbia. This heads up was furnished to my Canadian contemporaries, as well as all the border stations in the area. Our supposition was correct. One afternoon, within a week or so of the call, as I was looking toward the Peace Arch monument in the park from my window there the couple was. They were embracing under the Arch. Shortly after, they had made camp across Interstate I-5 near the railroad tracks on the west side of the Arch. It looked as though their tent and camping paraphernalia were almost straddling the 38th parallel, separating Canada from the United States. Naturally, we kept watch over this couple. They were stuck. One was not admissible to the United States and one of them was not allowed into Canada. Naturally, Canada was apprised of this couple. At least a week went by with this situation. Then they were up and gone! We never saw hide nor hair of them again. Possibly the male's threat was made in haste and in the heat of the situation and never to be acted upon. Who knows. One thing I can be almost sure of - they ended up either in Canada or the U.S. (in wedded bliss?)

Remember Al Capp's comic character Joe Btfsplk, the world's worst jinx, who had a perpetually dark cloud over his head? Well, one of the administrative clerks who had worked for me, could have been the female version of this guy. She wasn't quite so unfortunate though. To start her tale of woe, she informed me quite blithely upon her return from the post office one day with the office mail, that she had "mailed her purse." To begin with, she carried a quite large purse. Before I could question her about her problem, she informed me that she had actually put her purse in the pull-down drawer of the out-going mail (absentmindedly?) I am sure that the mail clerk must have been incredulous with her explanation. Anyhow, she got her purse back. And I never gave it another thought. Should this have been some sort of premonition of her?

The second incident that happened to her, and I might add almost did her in, she was T-boned at a local intersection in her car, due to her fault, I surmise, but I was never apprised where the fault lay. She was hospitalized for at least several weeks and off work for a month or so. No broken bones, but she had her spleen removed. Visiting her a number of times during her hospitalization, I thought she seemed more clear-headed than usual. Was it the medication they were administering to her?

Several months after her sick leave stint she spoke to me of her desire to apply for one of the trainee immigration inspector positions offered to aug-

93

ment our inspector contingent. I was not hesitant in telling her that her idea of applying for the trainee position was an excellent idea and I wished her the best in her endeavor. She was indeed selected as a trainee inspector for the Peace Arch station, and within a matter of several weeks she was on her way to Glynco, Georgia as an enrollee in IOBTC (Immigration Officers' Basic Training Course). Almost immediately, I filled the position she left. Our port immigration inspector trainee did not relay to me any difficulties she was having with her studies at the Academy. However, as I was later informed, she was not doing well, and in fact flunked! Apparently she did not make a passing grade on her mid-term examination, and it was physically impossible for her to make the grade at that point.

The telephone call from the District Director filled me in on all the details. Her travel arrangements were from the airport at Jacksonville, Florida. In her ineptitude or lack of awareness, absent mindedness, or whatever, she had left her carry-on bag where she had been seated, and departed the airport without it. Airport security found the bag she had left behind. Searching same for identification they found a personal amount of marijuana in the bag and a note from her girl friend to the effect that "toking" the weed should help her with her studies and the passing of her mid-term examination. Security called the Academy and thence the call from school to the District Director. I believe that the call from the District Director occurred on a late Friday afternoon. He informed me that she was to be brought to his office on Monday morning at 8:00 a.m. She was not to be informed beforehand of what had previously transpired.

Early the following Monday morning we were on our way to Seattle along with another female employee as a chaperone. When we arrived at the District Director's office in Seattle, he, with a very serious face, handed my inspector trainee employee a letter, a copy of which he handed to me. The gist of the letter read, that she was to be escorted to a particular physician's office whereby she was to furnish a urine specimen; a test for narcotics. If she failed the required test, appropriate remedial action would be taken. Otherwise, if she refused to furnish the urine specimen, she would lose employment with the Service. She opted not to submit to the urine test. Case closed. She was fired. Maybe the cloud over her head was self-induced. Just maybe she was high on marijuana when she mailed her purse, and when she was in the terrible car crash. She was replaced in her administrative clerical position at Blaine, by a transferee from another Agency. This one turned out to be an excellent employee.

It has been over thirty years since the transfer of the new employee, but I still remember vividly her phone call to me around 9:00 p.m. one evening. She matter-of-factly, but obviously under great shock, told me with difficulty that her daughter had been killed and that she would not be in to work the next day. I knew she had three children: A daughter in college (about 19), a boy (16), and a teenage daughter (about 13). I was at a loss of words but I know that I was extremely sorry and felt terrible for her. Her daughter in college was the first child about whom I thought she referred. But it turned out that it was not. As the murder story unraveled, my new employee's home was in the process of being robbed by her son, and his friend. While upstairs in her home, the alleged friend shot the young teen-aged daughter of my employee with her father's revolver (previously stolen) as she entered the front door. After fleeing the residence and arriving at a local teen drive-in restaurant hangout in Bellingham, the son called his mother. In a very short time the son and his friend were in police custody. The killer and co-conspirator were eventually tried as juveniles and sentenced to prison until their 21st birthday. The mother of the young girl who was shot eventually received a transfer to Seattle. Her other daughter who had been a college student at the time of the shooting, went on to law school and has been a practicing attorney for over 20 years. The son involved in the shooting (it was never proven he had fore-knowledge of the shooting) enrolled in college courses while in prison and as far as I am aware he has been successful in life since his release from prison years ago.

I knew that our Regional Commissioner from Saint Paul, Minnesota had an immense dislike for the Customs Service, and probably rightly so due to the fact that for years that Agency had tried on several occasions to gain control over inspections; in fact just a year or so before tried to do this politically but without success, which would make us, instead of equal partners, no more than second best at the least.

It just so happened that after a joint meeting in Vancouver, Canada in the early 1980s, we were all gathered in my office at the Peace Arch, including the Commissioner, his entourage, our District Director, and possibly one of my subordinate supervisors. The Commissioner asked me "what did Customs' supervisors wear on their epaulettes to designate their rank." Not sure what he was driving at, I said "they wear captain's bars, like my Immigration supervisors." As soon as possible, he said I want your supervisors to wear gold oak leaves, and as for you, I want you to wear a star

---

[26]They were eventually successful after 9/11. Now inspections control lies in Customs' hands. All inspections officers now wear the same uniform: Blue shirts and pants, bloused trousers, semi automatic weapons, mace, hand-cuffs, night stick, etc. The officers wear ball caps w/CBP (Customs and Border Protection) on the front.

when in uniform to designate your rank. Voila! I just got three newly minted majors as supervisors. As for myself I was knighted a brigadier general. Unfortunately, it did not come with extra pay! Within a year of our so-called promotions, the Regional Commissioner retired and our District Director was onward and upward, taking a promotion to a larger district in San Diego, California. Guess what? Immediately upon receiving this information I ordered a return to our previous rank designations; subordinate supervisors were to wear Captain's bars, and silver oak leaf (lieutenant colonel) would be worn by myself.

In 1981, Guru Rajneesh made a big splash in the Portland, Oregon District after his temporary admission into the United States for alleged medical treatment. No doubt he was the nemesis of the District Director in Portland. He was finally ousted from the United States after multiple hearings ranging for several years. He was arrested and deported on charges of immigration fraud as part of a plea bargain with U.S. officials.

We were affected by the ripple effect of the guru's admission after he established a so-called hippie ashram colony and moved it and his 93 Rolls-Royces to Antelope, Oregon, changing its name to City of Rajneesh, and advocated enlightenment through sexual promiscuity. His radical community attracted young people from all over North America, which obviously included, young, easily-impressed people from Canada. We, of course, experienced the consequences that occurred when large numbers of young people from Canada were refused admission largely due to the fact that they were immigrants without visas. In other words, they were unable to establish that they had employment in Canada, a compelling reason to return to Canada, and they did not have the necessary resources to come to the United States for an indeterminate amount of time to live in the commune at Antelope, Oregon (City of Ranjeesh).

An attorney for the guru Rajneesh called me to discuss the problem of all the young people being refused admission at Blaine, at which time I explained why they were not admitted. He was not satisfied with my explanation by telephone of the matter and wanted to discuss the issue face-to-

---

[27] The Administrative Manual clearly provides for captain's bars for GS-11 supervisors, and for GS-13 Port Directors silver oak leaf. The Regional Commissioner did not have the authority for any other designation.

[28] See Fort Worth, Texas Star telegram 1/20/90 for definitive discourse.

[29] His followers placed a red carpet from the doorway of the INS building to the hearing room so that his feet would not touch the unclean floor. Also, everything in the hearing room had to be sanitized. When it was mentioned that the American flag too had to be sanitized, the District Director blew his stack, off camera he thought.

face. Within a matter of days not only did the attorney for the guru show up at my office but Ma Anand Sheela, the Rajneesh's personal secretary, flying from Antelope in their private jet. Both of them were neatly caparisoned in maroon outer garments; I suppose the official garb of their group. I welcomed them into my office, shaking both their hands. We got right down to brass tacks. They didn't want to hear what I had to say, but it seemed that they listened attentively. They were unable to offer me any information that would change the course of my actions and those of the inspectors. The meeting probably lasted less than one hour, and when I stood up, an indication the meeting was ended, and as I held out my hand to bid them good bye, I was told politely that their beliefs did not permit the shaking of hands, but "we do this instead": they put their fingers together in front of them and bowed politely. I didn't participate in this ritual as I motioned at the door and said good bye.

In early 1981, the United States Public Health Service (USPHS) made an announcement that would be far-reaching as it affected the inspection and admission of aliens covering all the inspection activity of the Immigration Service. Since at least 1952 the Walter-McCarren Act provided for the exclusion or deportation of persons afflicted with psychopathic personality. Lumped into this group of people with mental problems were homosexuals. The edict by USPHS hit the major newspapers as well as the radio and television news. It wasn't before long before the Acting District Director from Seattle informed me personally of the need to immediately incorporate the USPHS news into action at the border. Basically he said, and I paraphrase, "Don't hassle persons with sexual orientation problems." His admonishment obviously did not include other individuals who had mental problems with Class "A" medical certification.

Closely following on the heels of the call from my superior in Seattle, I was interviewed in person by a reporter from a Seattle television station. In essence, I repeated what I was advised to say, which was that we no longer would be concerned about a person's sexual proclivity unless the individual made an issue of his same-sex identity. In the past, the exclusion of homosexuals did not make up a great portion of our statistics, but they nevertheless were there. Because of the large population center just north of us in the Vancouver, British Columbia area (nearly three million people) we did have our share of people of that sexual persuasion. Following my

---

[30]She later plead guilty to a number of charges, including "plotting to kill Rajneesh's physician with a poison-filled syringe and orchestrating a food poisoning outbreak that sickened more than 750 people in the Dalles, a plot to take control of the county.

policy, and before the brouhaha over the USPHS announcement, interviews to determine a person's admissibility was always done in a private manner, and particularly questions of personal sexual attribution. To the point, then questioning was not be in the line of sexual preference. That is not say, if an individual was blatant about his sexual orientation (wearing a T-shirt with I Am Gay emblazoned on it), thus making a formal declaration, he could and should be set-up for a hearing before an Immigration Judge. From the announcement from USPHS until my retirement I was not made aware of any problems, nor anyone being held for an exclusion hearing in light of this edict. Issue closed!

Prior to the Pope's visit to Abbotsford, British Columbia on May 1, 1981, we began to consider bracing for the onrush of persons visiting the Abbotsford site of the pope, who (U.S. residents) would be returning to the United States. The media, and particularly the printed media, in Vancouver, Canada, Bellingham, and Seattle, Washington took care of our problem. Headlines blazoned across the newspapers heralded the pope's visit but with one caveat: long traffic lines would dominate on Interstate 5 corridor in the direction north to the Abbottsford venue, and the waits at the Canadian border would take hours! The pope was greeted by thousands of people a good deal of whom lived in Canada, as the negative newspaper advice about the long waits and lines at the border had its effect on those aspiring U.S. participants. From the vantage point of my office overlooking the Peace Arch Park and Interstate I-5, I discerned the lack of hordes of anticipated northbound traffic, both the day before and early on the day of the pope's event. The media had done its job! This obviated my need to hold inspectors in overtime to cover for the deluge of cars that didn't happen. It was a non-event as far as inspections activity was concerned.

It was always enjoyable to get out of the office on details, particularly being on my own as an investigator made it difficult to be deskbound. Working on recruitment for the Border Patrol was a nice getaway. Recruitment covered Portland, Oregon and Seattle, Washington. I was a representative for Inspections in the Immigration Service, and the Chief Patrol Agent and one of his station seniors made up the three man team. We used the same questions that had been posed to me nearly 20 years before; asking about individual situations and evaluating how they respond to the answers was helpful in identifying and selecting future Border Patrolmen.

Nothing extraordinary happened at our hiring or non-hiring events, except two instances. In one case, while having coffee in the lunch room in Portland just prior to our interview, I happened to meet one of our prospective hires. Introducing ourselves, we discovered that he was raring to go.

There was a small glitch. The individual was legally blind! Shortly after in the interview room, the Chief already apprised of this fellow's anomaly, very curtly told him that he did not qualify because of his sight. The next day in Seattle we had scheduled a woman for interview, and she was late showing; considerably late, I might add. When she did show, her excuse was that she had car trouble! Anyway, before we got into the actual interview process, the Chief told her that officers occasionally encounter persons who are more than anti-Border Patrol, they are completely against law enforcement in general. In engaging in this explanation, he used some pretty vile language and he was right in her face with it. She became unglued, quite tearful and emotional. In his attempt to calm her down, he explained what we had to put up with again, and ask her if she was up to it. Shaking her head, she was asked to leave the room. It was a consensus of our board that she should be asked to withdraw her application and try again at another time. She agreed to take the Chief's advice. Maybe she tried again and was successful.

The year 1986 was a banner year for statistics. On May 1986 the World's Fair, Expo 86 open its gates on False Creek in Vancouver, B.C., Canada, which was to begin its five-month run until October of that year. Preliminary planning started almost one year previously with regular meetings with local law enforcement, mayors of the border cities, Chambers of Commerce, television and radio media et cetera and of course Immigration and Customs agencies from both sides of the border. Naturally, our planning included the interviewing and eventual hiring of extra staff and the same by our sister agency U.S. Customs. Obviously, training of the new staff was prioritized by all the agencies involved. The same agencies across the border, of course, had to beef up their staff.

Interviewing applicants for the exclusive period during the Expo 86 run from May 1986 to October 1986 was quite a task to say the least. We were furnished with a list of eligible applicants of 25 or so from our human resources department. The qualified people, all military veterans, according to the VRA (Veteran's Recover Act) were individually called in and interviewed. Since we are in the people business a good part of the personal interview was to determine if the individual had the necessary people skills and the temperament to conduct viable interviews, and being able to withstand mental abuse without going off the deep end. Obviously we were seeking temporary inspectors who were "people" persons.

Fortunately, the human resources department was aware that the hiring of these extra inspectors would take precedence and that the hiring process would need to be speeded up. Normally, a full-field investigation by the FBI would be required which would take months and months to accomplish.

While Patrolling Backwards

This full-field investigation was set aside for this special event only! Accordingly, we were mandated to contact by telephone each and every one of the applicant's personal references as supplied by the prospective employee to determine suitability and mental make-up for the job and the person's recommendation for hiring. Along with that, we also were required to check every position the individual had furnished on the SF 171, application for federal employment. There were no ifs nor buts about it, the prospective employee would be required to be "squeaky clean." No blotches on his employment record, and only a minor driving record could be sanctioned. There could be no equivocation by a personal reference nor an employer.

What a motley crew was finally selected with my recommendation to our District personal office. The only action after confirmation of their employment was a medical examination, to determine if they were physically able to perform their duties. Potential hirees included an air traffic controller, who with his contemporaries was fired by President Reagan, out-of work college graduates, a commercial artist with a masters degree and who was recently laid off by the local university, and even an individual with a previous occupation as bar tender (I caught some flak from the District Director on this one, but I stood my ground on this one, and he turned out to be one of our best inspectors, talk about a people person, an individual who was a full-time deputy sheriff who would
be hired for part-time employment, as well as several full-time teachers, who would come highly recommended for night and week-end employment. Included in my selection were also two local businessmen. Actually, all these temporary hires turned out to be top quality.

With additional staffing in place by both our agency and our sister agency U.S. Customs, we managed to handle the additional work load. The 1986 fiscal year, starting on October 1, 1985 and ending May 31, 1986 reflected that we had across our border at the Peace Arch (including the Pacific Highway) more than 10 million individuals. (Auto traffic was about 1/3 this total; a factor was used to determine the number of people). Of any problems that we encountered at all, they were minor. Never before in the history of this port did so many autos and individuals enter the United States. From Opening day May 2, 1986 to October 13, 1986 Expo 86 was the main contributor of the mass of people entering the United States during that period through the port-of-entry at Blaine. Of course, the Ports of

---

[31]The 1986 World Exposition on Transportation and Communication, or simply Expo 86 was a World's Fair was held in Vancouver, B.C., Canada - just 30 miles north of the Canadian I-99 and U.S. I-5 junction.

Lynden, Washington and the Sumas port-of-entry (the other ports of entry west of the Cascades) showed some traffic improvement too. The port at Blaine, though, was much more expedient since it was so close to the Expo site.

By appropriate staffing we were able to control southbound traffic to a great extent from Expo. Our Agency and U.S. Customs shared lane responsibility. During the week we could anticipate large amounts of traffic at around 6:00 p.m. and then again about midnight until 2:00 a.m., after the daily closure of the festival. During the above times, Immigration and Customs maintained maximum lane coverage at the Peace Arch. It was thought by most, including myself, that the enormous statistics generated by Expo 86 would be fleeting, and the following year traffic would return to normal. Wrong. There was a slight dip in figures in FY 1987, but thereafter in several years to come, until the extreme drop to .65 cents Canadian on the U.S. dollar in early 1990, traffic proliferated. It seemed like the Pacific Northwest had been discovered! Traffic elevated to pre-Expo days without doubt because of the condition of the Canadian dollar.

There was a rash of entrepreneurs in the Blaine city locales hoping to cash in on tourist dollars that were sure be from the visitors of Expo. Bed and breakfasts and the construction of an RV park at the north end of the city were the main endeavors. A rush was on to complete the Semiahmoo Resort across from the city of Blaine that never happened until 1987. A large cash flow into the investments at Blaine from Expo 86 failed to materialize. People visiting the Expo didn't slow down for Blaine but headed for points south on the Interstate 5. Possibly Bellingham, a short 20 miles down the road "trapped" some of the tourist money. How does one in my position, for whom "The Buck Stops Here" is so pertinent as the sign on President Truman's desk so aptly put, find encouragement and satisfaction with the job on a day-to-day basis?

Several things that gave me personal satisfaction were the pats on the back to individuals on a job well done; and especially to tangible awards such as certificates for outstanding performance with enhancement of monetary awards. Even length-of-service awards were accompanied by hardware to commemorate the event. I made it a point that all these events were publicized with photos in the local papers. One particular event that I recall, involved one of the inspector staff and his outstanding performance when he was responsible for the capture of the killer of a U.S. Customs officer. In recapping the event, the alleged killer had taken the life of a U.S. Customs officer in Toronto, Canada in an off-duty situation, and in the process stole the officer's auto. The whereabouts and direction of travel and destination of this killer was unknown, but a lookout blanketed all the

While Patrolling Backwards

inspections points, including the last northern border point, Blaine, Washington. Way before the introduction of computers, telephonic lookouts turned into paper Scotch-taped inside inspection booths. This particular lookout probably got lost in the shuffle after 3 weeks or so, since its involvement to begin with was nearly 3000 miles away! One of our officers had remembered the lookout and I wouldn't doubt that he didn't keep a copy on the same person. Anyhow, how fortuitous that the long arm of the law included such a dedicated inspector. Driving the deceased U.S. Customs officer, he showed up in the traffic lane of the dedicated inspector on my staff. His dedication to duty was commendable. In my office and in my presence, my inspector was recognized for his presence of mind and dedication to duty by a representative of the headquarters staff of U.S. Customs in San Francisco, California by the presentation of a plaque and a monetary award. What did me proud, was that this officer, who eventually became a full-time employee, had been interviewed and hired by me several years before.

I found what I called distasteful was the task of preparing letters in answer to complaints by travelers slighted in some way or other during the inspection process. Not cottoning to this process that I considered negative work, an interview was made of the inspector being complained about as well as a written memo covering his side of the complaint. I am not saying that my officer was always right; in fact, there were instances he was in the wrong. Nevertheless, I called this negative work because it called me away from more positive aspects of my job.

One particular day an alleged complainant called me to ask me if I could do something about a certain officer. It seems that the older lady, a bingo aficionado, on her almost daily trips to play local bingo when she was unfortunate enough to get this one officer, he would ask her to open her trunk but would never get out of the booth to check her empty trunk. She would get out of her car, open her trunk waiting for his appraisal that never came, and he would eventually tell her very officiously, to go ahead. To get to the bottom of this complaint I asked if she would, on her next trip to the U.S. and the same officer and circumstances prevailed to pull her over, come into the office, and ask for me. The very next day, a call from downstairs advised me that a lady was there to see me. Upstairs with the officer with whom she was unhappy, the officer denied any less than favorable activities attributable to him and the lady. The only thing he would admit to was seeing her quite often on her trips to the U.S. I had to admit it, but this officer was a known provoker. She must have set him off at one time. It was just a one on one situation. She said, he said, but I tended to believe the lady. It was my estimation that I was not hearing the full truth from the officer. Guess what. The lady was never bothered again by this officer.

It seemed as when I changed the performance work plan of the staff inspectors to include that the receipt of three or more work-related complaints (I was never challenged by the Union on what justifiable complaints meant) could mean termination of employment, complaints were almost negligible. My edict of "Look Good, Talk Nice, and Use Good Judgment," was in full force and effective. When I received a written complaint where the complainant didn't make a really good identification of the officer, a call to the traveler to determine if the officer wore a white shirt, with dress blue trousers or wore solid blue would alert me to either our agency or our sister agency. If the officer wore solid blue, I got the complaint off my back and referred the complainant to Customs. The tenor of my answer to a complaint was apologetic, never officious, and always ended that appropriate action would be taken. In this way, most of our complaints never made it any further that the port.

One afternoon a lady came into the office to register a complaint after having shortly before been inspected, and as she put it "rudely treated." Just inside the door of the building and the south end of the counter area she approached in a rather ruffled manner, seeking to vent her rage in the manner in which she had been handled by the officer on traffic. It is unknown which agency's inspector was at fault (outside), but a Customs officer met her face to face, and showing concern, asked her if he could help her. In a rather cold manner, she breathlessly unleashed her complaint. The Customs officer, a laid back, sympathetic employee, well-experienced, nonplussed, explained to her in a very calm voice, "Well, its like this, ma'am," he said, "We are an equal employment opportunity agency, and I sympathize with you, but we are required to hire a certain number of minorities, women, and rude people; it just so happens that you got one of the rude ones." Believe it or not, she got a smile on her face, thanked the officer and left. Talk about turning down the heat! The officer that got this lady to smile and change her disposition so quickly has never been the subject of a complaint that I am aware of. He was always 'cool as a cucumber' and a fine representative of his employer.

A complaint that came my way personally, occurred one Sunday afternoon. Working the counter this gargantuan individual, of Samoan ancestry, came up waving a referral slip, wanting to know what was going on. The referral slip had written on it, along with Immigration checked, the word SLOB. Not mincing his words, he wanted to know why the blank, blank officer outside called him a SLOB, and wanted his name. Not wanting to upset other customers in the vicinity, I asked him to come around the counter and come into the glassed-in office nearby so that we could discuss the matter in a more calm, gentlemanly environment. As I previously said, this guy was big, (like a professional football linebacker). First off, I apologized for any slight that he may have received, and explained to him that SLOB was an acronym we used and had nothing to do with his appearance (not to say that he was the most perfectly coiffed and nattily dressed person that I had ever seen). It seemed that I calmed his ruffled feathers and he accepted my apology and my explanation. After doing all the checks, which I found negative, he was on his way, seemingly satisfied. As a reminder to all inspectors, they were never to put anything on a referral slip of embarrassing or misleading nature. The mere fact that an individual is being sent inside for secondary inspection triggers an in-depth inspection including SLOB.

Another incident clouded my day when one of my officers asked that he and his wife meet with me for a personal matter. The crux of the matter was that my employee had recently been given the bad news of his impending misfortune when he was told by his physician that he had colon cancer. The likelihood of his living more than one year with this diagnosis was almost nil. If he had any male descendents age 40 or older they should be tested for that type of colon cancer, as it was genetic. Both he and his wife were unemotional, and in fact quite stoic about his fate. Married late in life, both were in their 50s. They had no children and family to speak of. His simple request was that his resignation be accepted. He just wanted to spend the rest of his days with his wife, spending as much time as possible doing things together. It was unnecessary for him to resign. Arrangements were made for him to retire under medical conditions. As his wish, he was able to spend his last days with his wife, for whom he had financially prepared when he died. Almost exactly, his life ended as the prognosis of the doctor was reality. He had a beautiful funeral, and since he had been a military veteran he was accorded the benefit of such and his wife was presented with an American flag that had been draped over his casket.

Not only was I going to miss him but also he would be missed by his co-workers and friends. I have no doubts that his presence was also missed by the traveling public. Having previously been a school teacher for over 16 years, he definitely was a people person, never ever having received a complaint of discourtesy. He was knowledgeable, quiet and laid back but he had a flair for his job. He was the epitome of what an immigration officer should be. He got along with everybody with whom he associated. Speaking with experience of this individual having known him for over 15 years, I know he left a void that could not be filled. There were times when he was assigned as acting supervisor that I knew his expertise showed through. I could always count on him in doing the best job possible.

While Patrolling Backwards

One day in a succession of mundane and immemorial events, things were going along quite smoothly when I received an official notification that I was being sued - along with the Area Director of Customs. About then I was wondering if I should have invested in a little law suit insurance like some of my contemporaries had done.

What brought this law suit on concerned a lawyer from Canada, who applying for admission one night was drunk out of his skull! Allegedly he had a fight with his spouse and was attempting to spend the night in their summer home in Birch Bay. He complicated things when he got into a drunken rage with the inspecting officers, was refusing to calm down, forcing the officers, both from Customs and Immigration to pile on him like he were a ball-carrying professional football player in the NFL. He ended up being hand-cuffed and settled into our station lock-up until he could straighten and sober up. Due to this ruckus and other extenuating circumstances He was denied entry into the United States.

Being a lawyer, a word merchant so to speak, he was to have his day in court - in fact U.S. District Court in Seattle, where the law suit was filed and to be settled. It would be pro se proceedings, which meant that he would be representing himself. The Area Director of Customs and I would be plaintiffs.

In court the Lawyer, in his arrogant way, had us both on the stand individually and questioned us both as to the how, why and when our officers had received their training in handling individuals who were simply exercising their rights to come to the United States. The judge could see right through this individual with his blathering and goings on and on with his raving and irrelevancies. On more than one occasion the judge called him down, and getting more impatient with him as time went by. Finally, without hesitation, the judge ordered the proceedings concluded. With a rapping of his gavel, he declared, "Case dismissed." Was the judge against Canadians, drunks or both. To paraphrase Abraham Lincoln, "A person who represents himself in a court of law has a fool for a client" was quite apropos in this case.

On a fateful, tragic late evening in early May, one of our young, up and coming inspectors was killed in a motorcycle accident. Just a few miles from home in Blaine, on a deserted two-lane country road, he failed to negotiate an almost 90-degree dogleg to the right turn while returning from Lynden, Washington where he had been enjoying an evening watching the Mariners baseball team play a game. His accident was not reported until the morning after, at least 10 hours later. Several of us were quite apprehensive around 8:00 a.m. the day following when he didn't show for work early on his day shift that he always did. While I usually walked to work, this morn-

While Patrolling Backwards

ing I was driving by his house around seven and I noted that it was strange that his motorcycle was not in the driveway. He hadn't shown for work either by the time I got to the station. He hadn't called in that he would be late and no one had heard from him. The inspector with whom he had enjoyed the ball game with last night was at odds with the matter, as he had last seen him when he had left Lynden. When the telephone rang about 8:30 a.m., those of us who had a premonition that was something was wrong and the call was probably concerning him. A sheriff's deputy was on the line asking if we could send someone out to identify an individual who had been killed on the Haney road, just east of town. His personal identity reflected that he was an inspector with our Service.

As it turned out, it indeed was Steve, our young inspector. The investigation revealed that he had been traveling on his motorcycle west on the Haney road, Just east of Blaine, failed to make a short 90 degree to the right, and continued straight ahead, leaving the roadway striking a large fallen tree, at which time his body was airborne for some distance, about 40 or so feet. The impact must have killed him. In checking the area and roadway a short time afterward, I am almost positive that the yellow caution sign 50 yards or so on the right hand of the road from the curve was missing. To this day, it is unresolved how this accident happened. Was it because his vision was impaired due to the foggy night, the missing warning sign, his speed, or his lack of familiarity with the road or a combination thereof? Indeed, he was on a less traveled road, but a shorter route from Lynden. The other two roads leading to Blaine were straighter but longer. It was heartrending to notify his father in up-state New York about his son's accident. The port where had been previously employed before his selection for transfer to Blaine not long before. After picking up his father and step-mother at the airport, at the father's request I took them by the accident scene prior to taking them to the memorial service. It has been over 20 years since this incident. I have always thought that this young officer would have done commendably in the Immigration Service.

Epilogue

On March 3, 1993 President Bill Clinton initiated an inter-agency task force headed-up by Vice President Al Gore, to reform and streamline the way federal government works. In creating the National Partnership for Reinventing Government (NPR) President Clinton said, "Our goal is to make the entire federal government less expensive and more efficient and to change the culture of our national bureaucracy away from complacency and entitlement toward initiative and empowerment." The NPR is not new. It is the eleventh federal reform effort in the 20th century.

For our agency, the United States Immigration Service, under the Justice Department, this grandiose scheme mainly the work of Vice President Al Gore, had its effect on me among countless others in the thinning of our ranks. In the early stages of NPR in 1993 our Regional Headquarters human resources staff in Saint Paul, Minnesota hinted of a "buy out" for retirement-age personnel. In other words, there might be a voluntary program for eligible employees to be paid a certain amount of money, thus reducing our ranks.

In mid 1994, rumor became reality and NPR came to fruition. Our regional office opted for the plan to thin its ranks and become more efficient and less expensive by offering the buyout program to its retirement eligible retirees (age 55 with 25 years service). On the band wagon I jumped as well as a majority of those elegible throughout the Immigration Service. What a break for me! I was only two years short of drawing the maximum 80 percent retirement anyway: thirty-three with INS years, plus four years military time and one year sick-leave, for a total of thirty-eight years. The only draw-back to this buyout retirement was that of my non-eligibility to come back temporarily as a re-hired annuitant should it become available. On June 2, 1994 my retirement became official and I never looked back.

Postscript

Sir Winston Churchill, Prime Minister of England during World War II and known by all as quite astute in his observations and the English language, once said, "The only thing permanent is change." Truer words could not have been better spoken, particularly in light of my perspective and experience during my career in the Immigration Service.

When I entered on duty with the Border Patrol at Chula Vista, California in the early summer of 1961 at the young age of 25, professional life could not have been more idyllic for me and my compatriots. Apprehensions were more or less static; a busy month in summer would show 400 to 600 apprehensions. We had only about one mile of ten foot cyclone fencing with concertina wire atop; the rest was 4-strand barbed wire fencing, which was mostly to keep cattle where they belonged. We had a sign-cutting shift (daylight to mid-afternoon), day shift, night shift, midnight to 8 a.m., city scout and bus station detail. No one really had to break their hump.

There was an Act promulgated during WW II called the Bracero Act, which was called for during the war to replace those men gone to war. The essence of the program was the U.S. government acted as go-between to screen employable-age Mexican males for ranchers and farmers to fill agriculture slots. There is no doubt that this program was useful and above all, necessary. Those selected were issued documentation, called an I-100C, which was good for the agricultural year. Politics had a great deal to do with the demise of the Bracero Act which was permitted to die in 1964. I would be remiss though, if I did not mention that the program was fraught with abuse and neglect.

We have also had temporary worker programs linked to the Canadian loggers in Maine and the cane cutters from Haiti and the Dominican Republic in Florida. Obviously, our powers to be could not see the inevitable coming, I.e., when the Bracero program was no longer. Ranchers and farmers still had the need for help, so consequently the once-legal the illegal's entered the U.S., more and more every year. Our resources and manpower were out-matched by the streaming hordes. While we had encountered 600 or so illegal's in a busy summer month in the 1960s at Chula Vista, those statistics climbed to over 2,000 during an eight-hour shift 20 years later.

Immigration started slowly changing with additions of manpower and resources. Gradually, laws were enacted to make it unlawful to hire persons not specifically authorized to work. Eventually, over eleven miles on the U.S./Tijuana border were substantially fenced to slow down the exodus from Mexico; consequently, the undocumented immigrants just crossed beyond the end of the high fence into the deadly desert, desperately seeking employment in the land of milk and honey. Yearly, Congress approved additional manpower.

Illegal immigration and its control has always been a contentious issue and a hot potato to handle politically. The somewhat lackadaisical attitude toward the admission of aliens and of what to do about the undocumented aliens in our midst harbored by our politicos came to a screeching halt on September 11, 2001 when over 3,000 innocent people were killed by Muslim terrorists who directed airplanes into the World Trade Towers in New York City, the Pentagon, and Bucks County, Pennsylvania.

It seems that money has been no object in curtailing any such thing happening again. We have now gone from about 900 plus Border Patrol officers country- wide (in the 1960s) to the more than 2,000 officers in The El Centro Sector alone. The Blaine, Washington sector, which at one time was without enough officers to man the midnight shift now has ten times more officers than pre 9/11. With increased manpower have come additional aircraft, boats and helicopters.

Inspections-wise, U.S. Customs has been granted the key role at all ports of entry: three inspections agencies (Immigration, Customs, Agriculture) that once held sway have now been melded into one agency under Homeland Security. All inspections officers now wear the same uniform: dark blue shirts and pants with all the accoutrements of enforcement officers: weapons, extra ammunition, handcuffs, mace, et cetera, and they are under the auspices of CBP (Customs and Border Protection) whose logo is emblazoned on their caps. They, of course, are responsible for the combined knowledge of the old U.S. Customs and the old Immigration Service.

U.S. Immigration investigations, of which I spent nearly five years of my Service career, is now a combined agency under Homeland Security, named ICE (Immigration and Customs Enforcement). Adjudications used to be a separate section of the Immigration Service. It is now called USCIS (United States Citizenship and Immigration Services). It appears that the U.S. Border Patrol is still a separate entity. Has the homogenized CBP been an effective unit? Probably. Only time will tell. At this time I see better traffic lane coverage than before. Also, shared intelligence information appears to be a plus.

An immediate answer to our illegal alien problem is not evident. Do we need to do something about it? Definitely yes. Figures range from ten million to twelve million illegal aliens (the numbers of documented aliens who have over-stayed and or worked without permission vary also).

Without doubt, some sort of an amnesty program (with a great deal of oversight) should be enacted. A more wieldy, less time consuming to obtain temporary worker program in concert with amnesty could be a viable alternative to the present situation, depending on available economic resources in the U.S.

About the Author

Andrew L. Hattery

Born in southwest Missouri in 1935 in the middle of the Great Depression, Mr. Hattery was witness to many changes during his tenure as a United States government civil servant. From his start in the Air Force, through his early years on the Tijuana, Mexico border as a Border Patrol agent to joining the United States Immigration Service (Inspections) and his first assignment; John F. Kennedy Airport - one of the busiest international airports in the country, to one of the small- est ports of Morgan, Montana. After Morgan, he was then given the assignment as immigration inspector at Blaine, Washington, then a promotion as criminal investigator in Omaha, Nebraska was next. And his final stint of sixteen years as Port Director, Blaine, Washington on the Washington/Canada border. Mr. Hattery regales us with his stories that will leave the reader laughing at times, bring tears to your eyes, but through it all you will gain a deeper understanding as to the sacrifices, compassion, and demands that are required in dealing with the public on a daily basis.

www.ingramcontent.com/pod-product-compliance
Lightning Source LLC
Chambersburg PA
CBHW071408290426
44108CB00014B/1737